From Quarantine to Q STATION

From Quarantine to Q Station

Honouring the Past, Securing the Future

ARBON
PUBLISHING

Published by Arbon Publishing Pty Ltd.
45 Hume Street, Crows Nest
NSW 2065, Australia
PO Box 623, Crows Nest
NSW 1585, Australia
Telephone: +61 2 9437 0438
Facsimile: +61 2 9437 0288
Email: admin@arbonpublishing.com
or visit www.arbonpublishing.com

Managing Director Fritz Gubler
Publisher Chryl Perry
Project Editor Dannielle Viera
Designer Stan Lamond
Picture Researcher Claudette Palomares
Proofreader Marie-Louise Taylor

National Library of Australia Cataloguing-in-Publication entry
Title: From quarantine to Q Station : honouring the past, securing
the future / Dannielle Viera, Jennifer Cornwell, Simon McArthur,
Peter Hobbins, Annie Clarke, Ursula Frederick.

Edition: 2nd edition.

ISBN: 9780994310736 (paperback)

Subjects: North Head Quarantine Station--Pictorial works.
    North Head Quarantine Station--Buildings--Conservation and
        restoration.
    North Head Quarantine Station--History.
    Quarantine--New South Wales--History.
    Isolation (Hospital care)--New South Wales--History.
    North Head (N.S.W.)

Creators/Contributors:
    Viera, Dannielle, author.
    Cornwall, Jennifer, author.
    McArthur, Simon, author.
    Hobbins, Peter, author.
    Clarke, Annie, author.
    Frederick, Ursula, author.

Dewey Number: 725.5099441

This book was printed and bound in China by
Toppan Leefung Printing Limited

Right: A modern staircase was built above the old funicular
track at Q Station.

Foreword

There is no doubt that the Public Private Partnership between the New South Wales Government and The Mawland Group at the old Quarantine Station, North Head, Manly (now known as Q Station) has given greater and more meaningful access to this site. This in turn has led to increased appreciation of its national significance by both the Australian community and tourists. The site's current incarnation also serves to secure its future as a viable and self-sustaining cultural tourism heritage site.

Today Mawland holds a long-term lease on the site, with a mandate to conserve and to operate it on behalf of the Australian people. Following Mawland's careful restoration and conservation of the Quarantine Station buildings, the site now looks much as it did in the 1920s, although aspects of both earlier and later periods of operation are evident.

Preserving and telling the stories of the many migrants and other past occupants of the old Quarantine Station has been a major focus of Mawland's adaptation of the site. Conserving the site has involved compliance with hundreds of policies and plans established by the New South Wales Government, with every piece of work or adaptation on the site clearly in accordance with best practice conservation methods and strictly overseen by the National Parks and Wildlife Service. Thus, improvements to and adaptive reuse of the site serve to protect its historic fabric, while Q Station's new functions serve to ensure its future.

I am particularly pleased that Q Station provides a unique environment in which to actively engage primary- and tertiary-level students with topics in History, Science, English, Art, Drama, PDHPE and more. Increased public access to the site gives locals and tourists alike the opportunity to witness the beauty of Q Station's indigenous, natural and cultural heritage and environment, including its native flora and fauna, with endangered or threatened animals, such as bandicoots, echidnas, little penguins, whales, dolphins and sea eagles, represented.

Ensuring that Mawland's reuse of this unique and precious site is both appropriate and beneficial to the people of New South Wales, who ultimately own the site, has also required the cooperation of the local community. I thank the Q Station Community Advisory Committee, which volunteers time to give community input into interpretation and public use of the site and to discuss ways in which the local and state community can access and receive education about Q Station's natural and cultural heritage.

Q Station has become a meeting point for the community. I congratulate Mawland on the publication of this book, which reflects its passion for the site while also commemorating its history and beauty.

Mark Speakman
MP for Cronulla
Environment and Heritage Minister

Foreword

I first visited the Quarantine Station in 1993. The day was cold, the sky was pouring with heavy Sydney rain, and the air was full of salt sea spray – and I was immediately overcome by the mystical presence of the site and knew that it would become a large part of my life.

Having just completed the redevelopment of a heritage site in the Blue Mountains, which was transformed into the luxurious Lilianfels Resort & Spa, and having established the Blue Mountains International Hotel Management School in Leura, it was tempting to have a long rest. However, I was exhilarated by the energy and potential of the Quarantine Station, and I felt that bringing it back to life would be an ideal way for me to leave some legacy to Sydney. My dream was to develop the site as an iconic hotel, conference centre and tourist attraction, so that Sydney residents and visitors could learn about and appreciate Australia's migration history, as well as the natural wonders of the site's special headland.

The Mawland Group lodged a formal Expression of Interest in the Quarantine Station in 1993, my obsession was born, and I quickly discovered that the New South Wales National Parks and Wildlife Service regarded the site as the jewel in their crown. However, I could not have envisaged the long process that would finally see the lease signed in 2006 – or that another two years would pass before we were able to host our first overnight visitor in 2008!

Mawland's conservation and adaptation project is now complete, and we welcome nearly 100,000 visitors per year to the site, leaving no doubt that it has been brought back to life under the Q Station banner, while Mawland remains an Australian family company.

Please enjoy this book about the history and future of wonderful Q Station, which is published as we enter the year of our tenth anniversary of lease operation. I am proud that Q Station is once again a functioning icon of Sydney Harbour, as well as a must-see destination for visitors to Manly – and I encourage you to visit the site and embark on your own journey of discovery.

Max Player
Managing Director
Mawland Quarantine Station

CAREFREE LIFE UNDER YELLOW FLAG
FEDERAL QUARANTINE
TRESPASSERS
PROSECUTED. PENALTY $25
S.S. ROGGEVEEN
JAN. 1928
BATAVIA

Contents

Sections of thick bushland have been retained throughout the Quarantine Station site, providing a safe haven for a wide variety of native birds and animals.

Eastern water dragons (*Itellagama lesueurii lesueurii*) are naturally found along Australia's east coast. Keen-eyed visitors to North Head may spot one sunbaking on a rocky outcrop.

Chapter 1

A Natural Place

The Quarantine Station Lease Area is located on North Head, a sandstone cliff towering 80 metres above sea level at the entrance to Sydney Harbour. It commands spectacular vistas across North Harbour, Port Jackson and the entrance to Sydney Harbour. North Head is formed from Hawkesbury sandstone and is covered by ancient Pleistocene-era sand dunes on which unique vegetation communities flourish. The limited access to North Head, due to its historical use for quarantine and present management as a national park, has minimised urban development in this area. As a result there is considerable biological diversity, including several rare plant and animal species, surviving within North Head and the Quarantine Station.

Diverse Landscape

The topography of the Quarantine Station is highly varied, ranging from sheltered flat areas above Quarantine Beach to steep yet heavily treed sandstone escarpments as well as open heath scrub on gently sloping exposed areas. This variation in topography influenced the establishment of the buildings on the site. The lower sheltered flat ground above the beach is protected from coastal winds and is well suited to arrival facilities. By contrast, the upper ocean-facing ridge lines are exposed to the coastal breeze. With fresh air thought to contribute to improved health, these provided an ideal location for the hospital facilities. The rolling valleys and ridge lines of the site supplied gentle gradients for road and pedestrian access, as well as sensational views across the harbour.

The Quarantine Station landscape comprises a diversity of ecological environments, including protected rainforest gullies near the harbour, ridge-top woodland on the ridge lines, bushland on the valley slopes, heath on the rocky outcrops and coastal escarpments and open heathland communities on the elevated, exposed and gently graded areas close to the Wharf Precinct. The variety of native plants and dramatic natural landscape fascinated those newly arrived to the Quarantine Station, and its beauty provided some consolation during their detention.

The variety of native plants and dramatic natural landscape fascinated those newly arrived to the Quarantine Station

⌃ The constant pounding of ocean waves against the North Head coastline has created rough vertical cliffs in the Hawkesbury sandstone.

⌄ The vegetation around the Quarantine Station varies from low-growing heathland to pretty wattles and gum trees (*Acacia* and *Eucalyptus* species).

Native Plants

The diverse vegetation communities that make up the remarkable Quarantine Station landscape contain a range of unique plants, some listed and protected by State and Commonwealth legislation. The sunshine wattle (*Acacia terminalis* subsp. *terminalis*), which has dark glossy green leaves and pale yellow flowers, is listed as endangered. Camfield's stringybark (*Eucalyptus camfieldii*), a small gum tree with thick, broad, almost circular leaves, is classified as vulnerable. The open heathland vegetation community known as Eastern Suburbs banksia scrub is listed as an endangered ecological community, and it historically covered an extensive area around Sydney Harbour.

Other plants that are found in the distinctive natural landscape of the site include large white-trunked broad-leaved paperbarks (*Melaleuca quinquenervia*); expansive Port Jackson figs (*Ficus rubiginosa*), which are present on the escarpments around the Wharf Precinct; and the diverse ground-covering flora, including carpets of flannel flowers (*Actinotus helianthi*) near the Former Isolation Precinct. There is also common heath (*Epacris impressa*) along the road above the Former First Class Precinct, and the large spreading red-fruit saw-sedge (*Gahnia sieberiana*), with its graceful brown seed heads, can be seen from the entry road into the Quarantine Station.

V The sunshine wattle (*Acacia terminalis* subsp. *terminalis*) has gorgeous yellow flowers in autumn. This shrub is found only in coastal areas around Sydney, including North Head.

The diverse vegetation communities that make up the remarkable Quarantine Station landscape contain a range of unique plants

➤ Visitors to the Quarantine Station in the warmer months may spot the pale grey–green leaves and snow white blooms of the flannel flower (*Actinotus helianthi*).

➤ All but wiped out elsewhere due to urban expansion, Camfield's stringybark (*Eucalyptus camfieldii*) is protected on North Head. Its seed pods attract small native birds.

➤ Aptly named, the broad-leaved paperbark (*Melaleuca quinquenervia*) has bark that sheds in papery strips. Aboriginal people used the bark to make shelter and food containers.

Native Wildlife

As part of North Head, the site provides habitat for a range of native wildlife, including small mammals, reptiles, birds and frogs. The most frequently encountered species include the common ringtail possum (*Pseudocheirus peregrinus*), the common brushtail possum (*Trichosurus vulpecula*), the short-beaked echidna (*Tachyglossus aculeatus*), the eastern water dragon (*Itellagama lesueurii lesueurii*) and the diamond python (*Morelia spilota spilota*), along with numerous birds. The little penguin (*Eudyptula minor*) colony at Manly and the long-nosed bandicoot (*Perameles nasuta*) population found on the Quarantine Station site have been listed as endangered and protected since 1997. The powerful owl (*Ninox strenua*) is classified as vulnerable.

From Quarantine to Q STATION

⌃ A protected species in Australia, short-beaked echidnas (*Tachyglossus aculeatus*) like to forage for ants and termites in logs and soil. They use their sharp claws to dig for insects.

◄ Floating like colourful pieces of kelp on the ocean current, weedy seadragons (*Phyllopteryx taeniolatus*) can be seen in the waters off Store Beach and Quarantine Beach.

◄ Wooden fences stop visitors to the Quarantine Station from disturbing little penguin (*Eudyptula minor*) nesting areas. Gaps at the bottom of the fences allow the little penguins to roam freely.

▼ Once known as fairy penguins, little penguins (*Eudyptula minor*) are the world's smallest species of penguin. They are the only penguins with nesting sites along Australia's coastline.

The little penguins (*Eudyptula minor*) that nest in rock falls and rocky shorelines around Manly Point and North Head, including the eastern side of Spring Cove and Quarantine Beach, now form the only mainland breeding colony of penguins left anywhere in New South Wales. They are highly sensitive to disturbance, so fences have been erected in the Quarantine Station Lease Area to limit visitor access, noise and sound. The penguin population is carefully monitored.

In order to provide greater protection for the little penguins (*Eudyptula minor*), parts of Sydney's North Harbour were declared a 'critical habitat' in December 2002 and listed as areas vital for the survival of an endangered species, population or ecological community. This designation imposes stricter controls over activities in areas that are known to be used by the penguins for nesting and travelling to their nests. The critical habitat covers Collins Beach, Store Beach, Quarantine Beach and the northern side of Cannae Point, extending some 50 metres out from the mean high-water mark to make it easier for penguins to get to nesting areas and to include seagrass beds that are likely to be important feeding areas. The land boundary of the critical habitat in Sydney Harbour National Park includes ridge-top areas where penguins currently nest or could potentially nest in the future.

The waters below the high-water mark from Grotto Point to North Head are also protected as part of the North Sydney Harbour Aquatic Reserve. Declared in 1982 and the only Aquatic Reserve in Sydney Harbour, it protects the seagrass habitat of the little penguin (*Eudyptula minor*) and weedy seadragon (*Phyllopteryx taeniolatus*), as well as the larvae of tropical fish and invertebrates that are brought south by the East Australian Current. Some of Australia's earliest marine specimens were collected from Spring Cove during the 1830s by Dr James Stuart, a superintendent at the Quarantine Station, and are held at the Australian Museum in Sydney.

▲ Conserving the Quarantine Station's natural heritage is vitally important, and there are many processes in place to ensure that native flora and fauna are protected at all times.

Common throughout the Sydney region up until the 1960s, long-nosed bandicoots (*Perameles nasuta*) have declined in numbers thanks to gradual habitat loss to urban development and its associated threats (including domestic animals and

vehicles). Bandicoots are nocturnal, living in burrows in the scrub during the day and foraging at night for food. Their habitat is mainly woodland, coastal heath and scrub across North Head, but they also like to forage at night in the open grassed areas of North Head and the Quarantine Station. Plantings of soft tussock-forming native grasses provide refuge areas for the bandicoots while they are foraging.

The long-nosed bandicoot (*Perameles nasuta*) colony at North Head is highly significant because it is an isolated population

▲ The size of a rabbit, long-nosed bandicoots (*Perameles nasuta*) dig small round holes with their front feet. They then use their sensitive snout to poke around in each hole, looking for tasty insects.

The long-nosed bandicoot (*Perameles nasuta*) colony at North Head is highly significant because it is an isolated population, separated from other groups of bandicoots by the urbanised land bridge in Manly. Scientists believe the population may be genetically distinct. These animals have been the subject of a number of scientific studies, and they are therefore an important reference group. In the latter period of quarantine operations, the population was studied as part of an initiative to develop a serum to treat or prevent tick bites.

Minimising Visitor Impact

The natural heritage of the Quarantine Station Lease Area is an integral part of the site's cultural landscape, and its management requires considerable resources and commitment. A great deal of effort goes into the minimisation of visitor impact upon natural values throughout the Quarantine Station site. Some of the measures in place are more obvious than others. Day visitor vehicle access is limited to an entrance car park, with a shuttle bus service into the site. Guest vehicle access is also limited. Similarly, the restaurant closes at 11 pm to reduce noise and light, and there is no amplified music outdoors. A minimal impact code is communicated to visitors by shuttle drivers, signs, porters and even guest compendiums.

The centrepiece of environmental management on the site is the Sustainability Policy and Environmental Management Plan, which is supported by noise, waste, landscape, bushland management, erosion and sedimentation control plans. The most innovative initiative is the Integrated Monitoring and Adaptive Management System (IMAMS). The IMAMS checks both the sustainability of the site and visitor activity on it.

▲ One of North Head's hidden gems, Collins Beach has a waterfall thanks to a creek that drains into Spring Cove. The beach was named after the First Fleet's Captain David Collins.

▼ Quarantine Beach is popular with visitors, especially during the warmer months of the year. Swimming, kayaking and other water sports can be enjoyed here.

⋏ This hand-painted aquatint by Joseph Lycett (c. 1775–1828) was published in 1824. It encompasses a picturesque view of North and South Heads at the entrance to Port Jackson.

➤ Aboriginal presence near modern-day Manly is revealed by these historical artworks located on Bora Rock, illustrated by naturalist James Samuel Bray (1840–1918) in 1891.

Chapter 2
Aboriginal Heritage

North Head is located at the entrance to Sydney Harbour, in the present-day suburb of Manly. There is little detailed knowledge of the Aboriginal presence at North Head prior to European settlement, but undoubtedly it was the site of some of the earliest contact and formative interaction between Aboriginal people and the British. On 29 January 1788, Captain John Hunter and Lieutenant William Bradley, from HMS *Sirius*, landed on what is now known as Quarantine Beach during an initial survey of the harbour following the arrival of the First Fleet in Port Jackson just three days earlier.

Aboriginal Presence

An 1820 engraving by convict Walter Preston (1777–18??) depicts the Aboriginal presence around the shores of Port Jackson during the early part of the nineteenth century.

The Cadigal were the Aboriginal caretakers of the eastern part of the shores south of Port Jackson. The tribal name of the Aboriginal people who occupied North Head is not known. It has been claimed that North Head fell within the territory of the Kuring-gai tribe. However, this Aboriginal tribal name does not exist; it was coined by a white man, John Fraser, in 1892. The local clan associated with North Head was the Gayimai. North Head was also used by the powerful *koradgee* (healers) of the Cameraigal clan for healing and burial ceremonies.

Hoping to learn more about Aboriginal customs and language to foster contact, Governor Arthur Phillip ordered the capture of a young Aboriginal man

CONTACT MADE

Hoping to learn more about Aboriginal customs and language to foster contact, Governor Arthur Phillip ordered the capture of a young Aboriginal man known as Arabanoo, at Manly Cove in December 1788. He soon lived freely in the Sydney settlement. In November 1789 another two Aboriginal men, Bennelong and Colebee, were also kidnapped from the same place. Both soon escaped.

A The taking of Colebee and Bennelong in 1789 was re-created in watercolour by HMS *Sirius*'s First Lieutenant, William Bradley (1757–1833), who supervised the capture of the men.

Governor Phillip was speared at Manly Cove the following year by Wil-le-me-ring, a friend of Bennelong, while he was trying to convince Bennelong to return to Sydney. This event led to Bennelong re-establishing contact with Phillip; Bennelong went to inquire after Phillip's health, and a personal relationship between the two of them soon developed. Bennelong became a regular visitor to Government House. Phillip had a hut built for him on what is now known as Bennelong Point, where the Sydney Opera House currently stands.

Bennelong went to inquire after Phillip's health, and a personal relationship between the two of them soon developed

▲ In 1792, Bennelong travelled with Governor Arthur Phillip to England, where he was dressed in European clothes so he could meet the king. He returned to Sydney in 1795, and died in 1813.

◄ Governor Arthur Phillip was ahead of his time. Despite being speared, he maintained a policy of tolerance towards Aboriginal people, insisting that they should be treated well.

From Quarantine to Q STATION

Impact of Introduced Diseases

The local Aboriginal people were the earliest victims of introduced diseases in the colony. Diseases such as smallpox swept through the local Cadigal communities, and by 1791 smallpox or a similar disease had killed a large proportion of the Aboriginal population around Port Jackson. Arabanoo was one of the many victims, dying in May 1789. Some clans almost disappeared. The disaster could have been prevented, or at least substantially minimised, had quarantine processes been in place from the time of the colony's establishment.

The Port Jackson clans lived on fish as well as animal and vegetable foodstuffs. Women fished from canoes with hooks of shell, fishbone or wood and lines of twisted fibre, while the men speared fish from rock platforms with multipronged gigs.

In a watercolour painting dated to c. 1817, Joseph Lycett (c. 1775–1828) shows two Aboriginal men using traditional spears to hunt for eels, an important food source.

Prior to the smallpox epidemic, canoes made from sheet bark turned up and tied together, in the centre of which were small fires on patches of clay or seaweed for warmth or cooking, were a constant sight on the harbour. The rocky shores and adjacent waves of the Quarantine Station site were frequented for the abundant seafood that was found there.

Preserving Aboriginal Sites

Physical evidence of the Aboriginal presence includes middens, rock shelters, artworks, open camp sites and burial grounds. Of the Aboriginal archaeological sites identified and recorded at North Head, over 20 are within the Quarantine Station Lease Area. It is likely that more are hidden by the vegetation and embedded in the soil below or around the buildings. Because of its use for quarantine purposes and management as a National Park after 1984 (which restricted public access to North Head), more Aboriginal sites have been preserved than would normally be the case in an urban area.

From Quarantine to QSTATION

The site of the former Quarantine Station is part of the rich history of Aboriginal occupation of Sydney Harbour and the wider district – and its Aboriginal heritage value is integral to its cultural significance.

RESPONSIBLE MANAGEMENT

The area continues to have great significance for the Aboriginal community, particularly because of its many burial sites. In 2002, Mawland Quarantine Station and the New South Wales National Parks and Wildlife Service signed an influential Memorandum of Understanding with the Metropolitan Land Council. This document deals with the means of consultation and shared responsibility for the conservation and interpretation of Aboriginal heritage associated with the Quarantine Station Lease Area.

Local Aboriginal people who are not associated with the Metropolitan Land Council also have the opportunity to advise on both site management and operations. They do this through representation on the Quarantine Station Community Committee, which was formed in 2004.

Augustus Earle (1793–1838) captured in watercolour the stark contrast between a simple Aboriginal canoe and the more sophisticated European sailing ships in Port Jackson in the 1820s.

➤ After enjoying several weeks at the Quarantine Station in *c.* 1935, when detainment was akin to a holiday camp stay, these visitors were given a clean bill of health and allowed to leave.

➤ Frightened Sydney residents living through the pneumonic influenza pandemic in 1919 attempted to ward off the germs by wearing surgical masks while they were out in public.

Chapter 3
History of the Quarantine Station

Before the development of modern medicine, infectious diseases posed a major public health threat. The only known means of protecting communities from outbreaks was to isolate sufferers and those with whom they had been in contact. For immigrants in the nineteenth and early twentieth century who had already endured the long voyage to Australia, quarantine could be a frightening and traumatic experience. Separated from healthy family members, those in quarantine had no way of knowing whether they would see their loved ones again. Some children left the Quarantine Station as orphans, and some women as widows, alone in a strange country with no means of support.

The Ideal Site

With its towering sandstone cliffs, North Head had been of navigational importance since the arrival of the First Fleet. It was first used as a quarantine area in 1828, when convicts and guards from the *Bussorah Merchant* landed at the site because there had been a smallpox outbreak during the voyage.

Just five years later, in February 1833, North Head was officially reserved for quarantine purposes to minimise the risk of importing diseases to the infant colony. The site was selected because it had a deep anchorage in Spring Cove, beaches suitable for landing and airing cargo, a fresh water supply from the swamp ground above Quarantine Beach and remoteness from the Sydney settlement.

Early Quarantine Practices

Vessels carrying cases of disease were initially isolated and anchored offshore within Port Jackson until medical officers deemed there was no longer any threat of disease to the local settlement. Quarantine was imposed by order of the governor of the day. The system worked well while the majority of vessels arriving in Port Jackson were convict ships. The growing number of commercial vessels entering the port from the 1830s, together with large-scale assisted immigration, made quarantine by proclamation increasingly difficult to enforce.

Based on a ship captain's drawing, this lithograph by William Spreat (1816–97?) shows North Head and the quarantine ground in the first half of the nineteenth century.

The masters of commercial vessels planned a quick turnaround in Port Jackson; passengers were disembarked and the ships loaded for the return voyage with a cargo of wool, tallow or whale oil. As any delay meant loss of income, any infectious diseases on board were likely to be concealed.

THE PLIGHT OF THE *LADY MACNAGHTEN*

Noncompliance by the ships' masters with the system of self-reporting infectious diseases led to the passage of the *Quarantine Act* in 1832, which made it mandatory for all ships to fully disclose diseases, and authorised the establishment of places for the purposes of quarantine. By then the landing of those on board quarantined vessels was becoming the established practice. It would take the 10-week quarantine of the *Lady MacNaghten* (which was mainly carrying assisted Irish immigrants) before the colonial government conceded that the arrival of large numbers of immigrant ships warranted a permanent station at North Head.

When the *Lady MacNaghten* arrived in Sydney in February 1837, there were at least 90 cases of typhus fever on board. Some 54 deaths from varying diseases had already occurred during the voyage. Under the quarantine arrangements, the sick remained on the ship, and healthy passengers were landed on the shore and accommodated in tents. The sick were finally transferred to shore in the third week of March.

▲ Those from the *Lady MacNaghten* who died from typhus fever were buried in the First Cemetery, which was located on the southern slopes above Quarantine Beach.

A Permanent Quarantine Station

Following the heavy *demurrage* (monetary compensation for the delay of a vessel in port) claimed as a result of the

lengthy detention of the *Lady MacNaghten,* and to minimise any costly future disruption to trade and commerce, the practice of landing the sick and fumigating and scouring the vessel for a quick return was formally adopted. Work on the construction of a permanent quarantine station with up-to-date facilities at North Head commenced in October 1837 and was completed by May the following year.

The practice of landing the sick and fumigating and scouring the vessel for a quick return was formally adopted

The Quarantine Station's First Cemetery, seen here in a coloured engraving by Arthur Willmore (1814–88), was used from 1837 until 1853. As it was situated within sight of the Healthy Ground, it caused great distress.

A wharf was built at Quarantine Beach for the landing of passengers and stores, and the high ground was divided into two sections: the so-called Healthy Ground for contacts above Quarantine Beach, and the Sick Ground located on the promontory area to the south and closer to the shore. A hospital with accommodation for 32 patients was built on the Sick Ground. Four wooden unlined buildings, each housing 25 people, were built on the Healthy Ground. Although quarantined immigrants complained about the lack of comfort and privacy, the accommodation standard reflected the official view that it should be equivalent to that of the ship – that is, steerage class.

The path leading to the Healthy Ground in the 1800s rambled up a steep hill, through dense bush. Visitors had to watch where they were treading, to avoid tripping on loose rocks and uneven ground.

From 1837, the Quarantine Station's boundary was marked by around 12 stone cairns, which were lime washed for visibility. The cairn seen in the far left of this photograph is the only one left standing today.

Medical checks and smallpox vaccinations became mandatory for all prospective emigrants

▲ Peter McNeil was one of 12 people from the *Minerva* who died at the Quarantine Station in 1838 after contracting typhus fever.

The Station's quarantine zone was delineated by some 12 or 13 stone cairns extending across the high ground. The boundary line this created was patrolled by a military guard encamped near Store Beach, and the quarantined were prohibited from passing beyond this point.

However, the Station's capacity fell far short of quarantine demands. In 1838 alone, five immigrant ships were quarantined – largely as a result of the appalling conditions on board the ships. A review of the conditions aboard immigrant vessels and the selection of British emigrants was conducted by the colonial government in late 1838 and led to reform of the system. Medical checks and smallpox vaccinations became mandatory for all prospective emigrants, together with improved diet, sanitary arrangements and hospital accommodation during the voyage. These changes saw a marked fall in quarantines.

◄ From the mid-1800s, the landing jetty at Store Beach was used by ships bringing provisions to the Quarantine Station. Nearby was a boatman's quarters.

➤ The one remaining stone cairn at the Quarantine Station site is located close to the Former Second Class Precinct. Next to it is an old wooden navigation beacon.

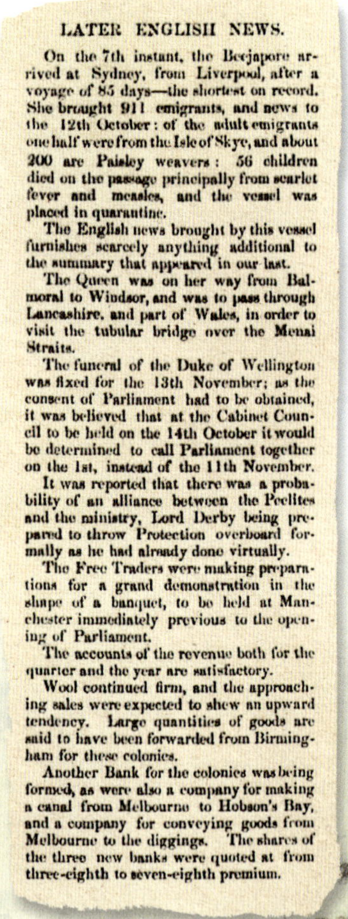

LATER ENGLISH NEWS.

On the 7th instant, the Beejapore arrived at Sydney, from Liverpool, after a voyage of 85 days—the shortest on record. She brought 911 emigrants, and news to the 12th October: of the adult emigrants one half were from the Isle of Skye, and about 200 are Paisley weavers: 56 children died on the passage principally from scarlet fever and measles, and the vessel was placed in quarantine.

The English news brought by this vessel furnishes scarcely anything additional to the summary that appeared in our last.

The Queen was on her way from Balmoral to Windsor, and was to pass through Lancashire, and part of Wales, in order to visit the tubular bridge over the Menai Straits.

The funeral of the Duke of Wellington was fixed for the 13th November; as the consent of Parliament had to be obtained, it was believed that at the Cabinet Council to be held on the 14th October it would be determined to call Parliament together on the 1st, instead of the 11th November.

It was reported that there was a probability of an alliance between the Peelites and the ministry, Lord Derby being prepared to throw Protection overboard formally as he had already done virtually.

The Free Traders were making preparations for a grand demonstration in the shape of a banquet, to be held at Manchester immediately previous to the opening of Parliament.

The accounts of the revenue both for the quarter and the year are satisfactory.

Wool continued firm, and the approaching sales were expected to shew an upward tendency. Large quantities of goods are said to have been forwarded from Birmingham for these colonies.

Another Bank for the colonies was being formed, as were also a company for making a canal from Melbourne to Hobson's Bay, and a company for conveying goods from Melbourne to the diggings. The shares of the three new banks were quoted at from three-eighth to seven-eighth premium.

▲ A lengthy article in Launceston's *The Examiner* newspaper from 20 January 1853 notes the *Beejapore's* quarantine before diving into the news the ship brought from England.

Growth in Immigration

Convict transportation ended in 1840, and with it the supply of labour to the colony. An economic downturn in the colony led to the virtual cessation of assisted immigration from late 1841 until 1847. The Quarantine Station fell into disrepair during these years. It was not until after the quarantining of the ill-fated *Beejapore* in January 1853 that steps were taken to substantially increase and improve accommodation at the Station. The two-decked vessel was chartered as part of an experiment in reducing migration costs. Fifty-six people had died during the voyage, mostly from measles and scarlet fever, and another 62 died at the Quarantine Station.

Most of the 1000 passengers and crew on board the *Beejapore* had to be housed in one of the 90 tents in the height of summer. It was not just the accommodation that came in for criticism. In a letter to the Colonial Secretary, a passenger called TR Miles attributed the death of his 18-year-old daughter, Gabriella, to the very poor standard of medical treatment.

A major upgrading of the Station's buildings followed, which increased its accommodation capacity from 150 to 450 persons. Those suffering from disease were now placed on a hospital ship, the hulk *Harmony*, moored in Spring Cove. A new burial ground (the Second Cemetery) was also established out of sight in bushland behind the Healthy Ground buildings.

▲ Thomas Convoy, from the *Smyrna*, was just four years old when he succumbed to scarlet fever and was buried in the Quarantine Station's Second Cemetery in August 1878.

▼ The *Harmony*, depicted in this pencil-and-wash drawing by George Penkivil Slade (1832–96), served as the Quarantine Station's hospital ship from 1853 until it was replaced by the *Faraway* in 1877.

INTRIGUING DIARY

The 375 immigrants and crew aboard the *Constitution,* which arrived from Southampton in May 1855, were among the first to use the improved Station, where they were quarantined for 65 days. One passenger, Charles Moore, kept a diary that provides some insight into the quarantine experience. Moore describes how the men had to carry the luggage up the sandy stone slopes in the heat to the single men and married quarters on the Healthy Ground. These buildings were unlined and had no ceilings, and, according to Moore, they looked 'just like a barn inside' although everything was 'clean and nice'.

But death was ever-present. Moore recounts one occasion when the *Harmony* hospital ship's bell tolled following the death of 'the poor woman that was locked jawed'. Those on the Healthy Ground had to 'keep back while the Corps came up the hill' on the way to the Second Cemetery, which was out of bounds. Her daughter died two days later, and was 'buried in a rasin [sic] box'.

Moore also describes how the corpse of a young woman sewn up in a blanket was carried up the slopes and past the buildings on the Healthy Ground for interment in the Second Cemetery. A bell had been rung on the ship as a warning to the quarantined to keep their distance while this took place. As boredom and the lack of privacy set in, Moore wrote that 'we are getting tired of this place'.

As commercial activity in the colony grew and maritime traffic increased, the Station was also used for the quarantine of non-immigrant vessels, including traders, mail ships and warships. Such use was generally limited to the Station's cleansing facilities, as it had come to be regarded as a place for the quarantine of assisted immigrants. Crew members of non-immigrant ships who were suffering diseases probably remained in their own bunks, although the rate of infection among this group was nowhere near as high as that of the immigrants.

From Quarantine to ℚ STATION

1855
1905
ALD J. BRIND
WALTER OATES
Wᵐ SAUNDERS
FRED. R. BRETTNAL
CHAS ADAMS
MRS Wᴹ HARE, SENᴿ
GEO. BRETTNAL
Tᴴ OATES
Mᴿ & Mᴿˢ PROCTOR
Mᴿ & Mᴿˢ HORNER
Wᴹ J. MILLS
Mᴿ T. KING
Mᴿ P. NICOLLE
W. LAYTON
Mᴿˢ M. ROULSTON
J. TAYLOR
Mᴿ & Mᴿˢ J. BOYCE
FRED OATES
Mᴿ COCKS
H. PURTON.   J. ADAMS.

This Memorial
WAS ERECTED
BY THE PASSENGERS OF THE
SHIP "CONSTITUTION"
WHICH ARRIVED 31ᵀ MAY 1855.
IN MEMORY OF THOSE WHO DIED
ON THE PASSAGE. ALSO THOSE
WHO DIED AFTER ARRIVAL.
THESE TABLETS
WERE PLACED HERE BY THE ABOVE
NAMED SURVIVING PASSENGERS
TO COMMEMORATE THE JUBILEE
OF THEIR ARRIVAL AND A REUNION
HELD ON THIS GROUND
ON THE FIRST EMPIRE DAY.
24ᵀᴴ MAY 1905.

THE ILLUSTRATED SYDNEY NEWS

AND
NEW SOUTH WALES
AGRICULTURIST & GRAZIER

Published every Four Weeks, or Thirteen times a Year. Annual Subscription, 9s., post paid.

No. 2—Vol. IX. FRIDAY, AUGUST 2, 1872. Price (with two Supplements) 1s.

NOTICE.

Our NEXT ISSUE will be a DOUBLE NUMBER, price One Shilling, containing a large

MINING AND GENERAL
MAP OF N. S. WALES,

printed in colours, and showing all the principal Towns, Distances, Roads, Rivers, Railways, Counties, &c., all Mineral Localities up to latest date.—Gold, Silver, Tin, Lead, Copper, Iron, Coal, Kerosene Shale, Salt, Precious Stones, Antimony, Manganese, Marble, Slate, &c.

This will form one of the best Mineral Guides procurable—as also a Map of general interest to all.

Country Agents and others desirous of securing extra copies are requested to make application at once.

QUARANTINE AND VACCINATION.

Since the first alarming intelligence reached our shores that Small-pox had obtained a footing in our colony, the Government have made indefatigable efforts to impede its progress and stamp it out ; but the ultimate success of these efforts still remains a matter of conjecture. Vessels arriving from infected ports have been placed in Quarantine with commendable zeal—too commendable,

perhaps, in the opinion of those passengers who are *not* infected, and who, consequently, have plenty of scope for the exercise of that gentle virtue, Patience, which is so much exalted theoretically, and so universally ignored practically.

All our dead-walls and hoardings have assumed quite a jaundiced aspect, on account of the prevalence of Quarantine Laws and Notices, printed on sulphur-coloured paper, and posted thereon ; and doubtless the bill-sticker's account will form an imposing item, over which some sagacious "Member" will immortalise himself on the subject of "retrenchment." Liberally, indeed, have the Government "hung out their (yellow) banners on the outward walls," and dire are the penalties to be inflicted on those who transgress the laws of Quarantine ; but with all this severity, care, and vigilance, Quarantine presents but a sorry barrier to the ingress of disease. There are so many ways in which its provisions may be eluded, and yet the offender escape detection,—so many means by which infection may be conveyed despite the strictest watchfulness, that Quarantine cannot be regarded as a reliable preventive to the outspreading of disease. There are distempers, it is true, against the introduction of which nothing can be placed as a barrier except the law of Quarantine most rigidly observed ; but it is not so in the case of the enemy against whose ingress we are now contending.

Our bane and antidote are both before us—

our bane, the dreadful Small-pox ; our antidote, Vacci-

nation. In the case of this insidious disorder (which may well be likened to a serpent stealthily creeping into our midst) Quarantine but "scotches" the snake, Vaccination kills it.

At a time, in years gone by, when Small-pox carried off more than 200,000 victims annually, and when it pleased Providence, in its own good time, to put it into the heart of man to discover and make known a preventitive, the discovery was not only ridiculed but denounced by press and pulpit. In an unenlightened age such absurdity is not to be wondered at ; but how people in the present day, fully informed on the subject, and cognizant of the triumph of Jenner's discovery, can refuse to avail themselves of such an invaluable boon, we are at a loss to fathom. There are some, we are aware, who reject it on the ground that other disorders are communicated through the medium of vaccine lymph, but universal medical testimony shows such instances to be extremely rare ; and with that caution which every honest medical man would exercise in the selection of lymph, there is scarcely a possibility of disease being introduced.

It is quite time that such stolid prejudices should be given up—prejudices which are not only productive of hurt to those who entertain them, but which lead to the spread of death and desolation among the community at large. It is quite time, when people will not voluntarily accept so beneficial and providential a measure, to make their acceptance compulsory, if only for the protection of those amongst whom they live.

QUARANTINE STATION, PORT JACKSON.

Segregated Accommodation

When the colony's assisted immigration program was again suspended during the 1860s and 1870s due to a stagnant economy, there was little use of the Station's accommodation – at least by steerage-class passengers. The advent of steam-powered vessels shortened the trip from Europe to Australia, which encouraged more affluent people to make the journey.

Ships carrying larger numbers of first-class passengers soon began to arrive in the colony. While there was an obvious class division on board ships, the Quarantine Station accommodation did not make any such distinction. The complaints of several influential people travelling in first class on the *Hero* in 1872 and the *Baroda* in 1873 prompted a quick response from the government. By 1876, the construction of accommodation suitable for first-class passengers had been completed.

Several staff cottages were built at the Quarantine Station over the years. Known as S5, this particular house was constructed in 1870, and it still stands today.

The Illustrated Sydney News and New South Wales Agriculturist & Grazier from 2 August 1872 details the ongoing need for quarantine and vaccinations.

Changing Quarantine Practices

➤ The Wharf Precinct was remodelled in 1883, when a steam laundry, coal shed and steam-operated fumigation sheds were built. A concrete pier replaced the wooden jetty.

▲ During the smallpox epidemic, policemen forcibly removed both sufferers and contacts from their homes. Detainees travelled from Woolloomooloo to the Station by steamer.

➤ By the late 1870s, there was a 22-bed hospital for males and a 12-bed hospital for females. In 1886, a new two-ward hospital was constructed (seen here in the background).

During the smallpox epidemic of 1881–2, the Quarantine Station was used to isolate Sydney residents; 104 Sydneysiders were forcibly detained between June and September 1881 alone. The Station was ill equipped to handle the quarantine of smallpox sufferers, and reports of horrendous neglect and substandard medical care quickly emerged. As criticism mounted, a Royal Commission was set up to inquire into the management of the Station. Its findings led to a number of important reforms, including the establishment of a central body to supervise the administration of public health measures. The Board of Health was then created in January 1882 as a branch of the New South Wales Department of Public Health, and its numerous responsibilities included quarantine.

That same year, the colony's detention-based quarantine regulations came under renewed criticism by shipping agents and owners, who urged the colony to follow Britain's lead. The costs of maintaining quarantine establishments, the disruption to shipping caused by detaining vessels and claims for *demurrage* had led to a shift away from detention-based quarantine in Britain and its eventual abandonment in 1873.

The colonial government, however, resisted pressure to follow suit. Steamship navigation had reduced the length of the voyage to Australia and the period for infectious diseases to manifest themselves, which had served as a natural barrier. Instead, it was decided to improve the Quarantine Station, including better landing and cleansing facilities at Spring Cove wharf and extension of the hospital and passenger accommodation. The Third Cemetery had already been established in September 1881. By 1889, immigrant ships carrying 600 passengers could be cleaned, disinfected, washed and admitted to pratique within 36 hours of arrival, and a steam laundry, baggage disinfector and baggage store were in operation in the Wharf Precinct.

Many professional rat-catchers were hired by city officials, and they were paid up to six pence per dead rat. Thousands of rats were killed and burned in special incinerators.

Advances in Public Health

The threat of bubonic plague highlighted the need for a Federal approach to disease control and prevention. During the late nineteenth century, this disease was being carried along sea routes by plague-infested rats and was spreading fast across the world. The quarantine barrier in Sydney was broken when rats escaped from moored vessels to the Darling Harbour wharves. The first case of bubonic plague appeared in January 1900; it was the first of 12 outbreaks in Sydney between 1900 and 1925.

Cleansing measures on quarantined vessels arriving in Australia were based on the advice of an 1897 International Convention that discounted the role of rats as carriers. In April 1900, the government's Principal Assistant Medical Officer discovered the plague bacillus in fleas on dead rats in Sydney, leading to rat-catching and cleansing operations in the city. The plague epidemic had proven that infectious diseases could be transmitted by insects and spread by animal carriers. As a result, public health measures and practices were altered to reflect this discovery.

Against the advice of the Board of Health, the government decided to use the Quarantine Station and not the Coast Hospital (which had been opened in December 1881 to deal with infectious diseases) for the isolation and treatment of all plague cases. Between January and August 1900, 264 plague cases and 1832 contacts were quarantined. Of the 103 victims of plague buried at the Station, 48 had died in Sydney and their bodies taken there for burial. In stark contrast to the smallpox quarantine, patients were well cared for, despite the enormous stress and long hours endured by the staff.

The plague epidemic had proven that infectious diseases could be transmitted by insects and spread by animal carriers

▼ Medical staff are photographed in the Hospital Precinct, c. 1900. Staff numbers swelled greatly during a quarantine emergency to include doctors and nurses, as well as cooks, laundresses and others.

➤ This is the interior of one of the Station's hospital wards during the plague epidemic. Netting hangs above the beds, as the site was notorious for mosquitoes in summer.

◄ Like many other narrow and dirty roads in Sydney in 1900, Wexford Street had tonnes of rubbish removed during the plague scare. This entire street was later demolished.

◀ The *Australian Town and Country Journal* pictured the Quarantine Station's wharf and cleansing facilities (middle) and hospital (left) in February 1900.

▼ In 1909, the Station's Third Class Precinct comprised 12 buildings. Nine of these were later demolished as the number of people held in quarantine became fewer over time.

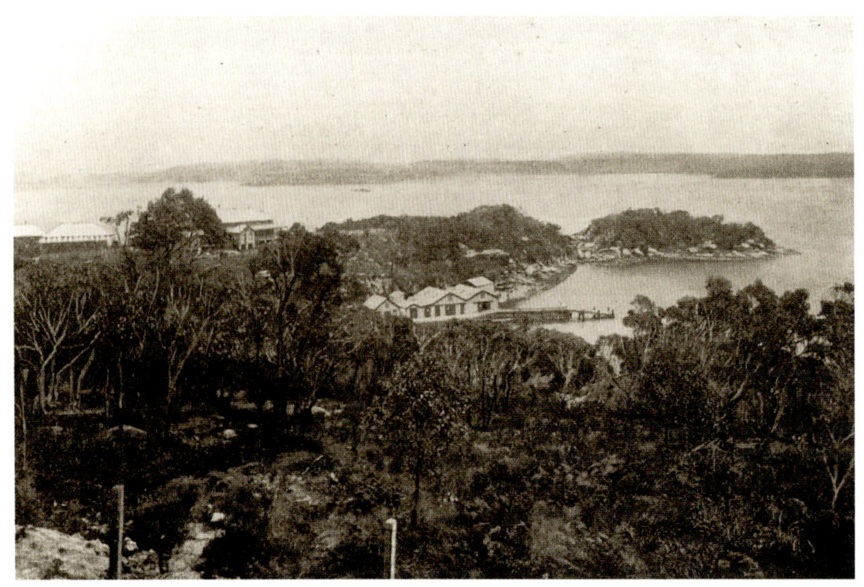

A major factor in the delay [of the Commonwealth takeover of the Quarantine Station] was the New South Wales Government's reluctance to relinquish the Station for fear of further land epidemics

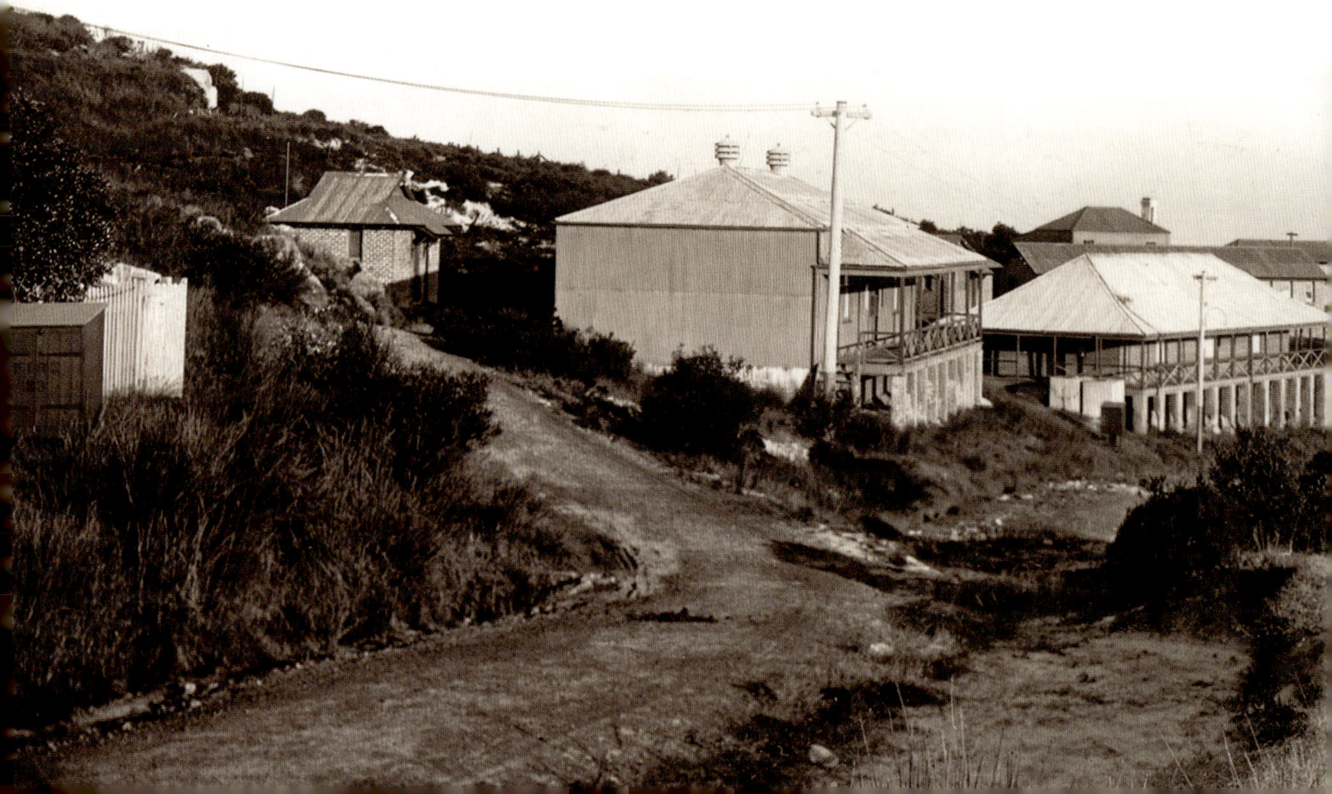

Transfer to the Commonwealth

Responsibility for quarantine and immigration passed to the new Commonwealth Government upon Federation in 1901. However, the new *Quarantine Act* did not come into force until July 1909, when quarantine stations all over Australia were taken over by the Commonwealth, with the actual transfer of the North Head Quarantine Station site not occurring until 1911. A major factor in the delay was the New South Wales Government's reluctance to relinquish the Station for fear of further land epidemics.

By that time, many overseas vessels with infectious diseases on board were quarantined at other stations before they arrived in Port Jackson. Between 1901 and 1912, most vessels quarantined at North Head were only detained for a few days for cleansing or the vaccination of passengers.

Further improvements were made to the Station in the years immediately prior to its transfer. Two pavilions were constructed to provide additional accommodation for contacts held on the Healthy Ground during the 1900 plague epidemic. Known as the Lyne's Buildings (named after the Premier of the day), they were completed in 1901. The plague was over by then, and they were converted for use as second-class accommodation. The older quarters in the southern area then became accommodation for third-class passengers.

▲ Each of the two Lyne's Buildings was simple in design, with weatherboard cladding and a corrugated iron roof. The iron sheeting was later replaced with concrete tiles.

Built in 1902, the 'Asiatic' accommodation consisted of army-style dormatories with bunk beds. Simple shared bathroom facilities were located at each end of the building.

In the following year, dedicated 'Asiatic' accommodation was built on the Healthy Ground, imposing yet another layer of classification on the site – that of race. First requested by the Shipping Owners' Association in 1882, it was a tangible expression of the White Australia Policy, underpinned by the desire to maintain the social and racial 'purity' of the population's British stock and enshrined in the Commonwealth *Immigration Restriction Act 1901*.

It provided basic bunk accommodation for 60 people; an open shed furnished with a log table, some stools and rice boilers served as the kitchen and dining area. The Chinese were often identified as the source of disease in the community and received scant treatment in quarantine. Reflecting the low regard for the comfort and welfare of this group of passengers and crew, the accommodation was still considered suitable in the 1930s despite its rundown state.

The Chinese were often identified as the source of disease in the community and received scant treatment in quarantine

TESTING THE FACILITIES

The first serious quarantine following the Commonwealth takeover of the Station was a smallpox epidemic in Sydney in 1913, believed to have originated from a crew member of the *Zeelandia*. The disease quickly spread throughout the mostly unvaccinated population, and an epidemic was proclaimed in July 1913. Between then and the end of January 1914, 1042 people were quarantined at the Station. At the peak of the epidemic, 309 people were housed in the wards and tents erected in the overcrowded Hospital Precinct.

SMALLPOX.

LIFT THE QUARANTINE.

HEALTH BOARD APPEAL.

There were five new cases of smallpox yesterday—three men and two women. Four of the cases came from one house in Surry Hills. The other was from Erskineville.

The statement of the Premier that the present outbreak is not one of true smallpox apparently resulted in the vaccinations in the city declining from 778 on Tuesday to 561 yesterday. The total vaccinations yesterday were 669—561 at the Town Hall, and 108 at Cockatoo Island.

There are 70 patients and 238 convalescents at the Quarantine Hospital. Thirteen cured cases were released yesterday.

The resolutions of the Board of Health, on which the Premier based his statement, are in the following terms:—

That the Board of Health has now at its disposal the experience gained by its medical staff in seven hundred (700) cases of smallpox, which have occurred during the present epidemic in Sydney.

The board is satisfied from such experience that the disease now present in Sydney is an exceedingly modified form of smallpox, mild in its nature, and with no tendency to change its type and become more virulent, and in this view they are supported by the writings of Castellani, Chalmers, and others.

That the danger of it becoming epidemic in the other States of the Commonwealth is negligible, seeing that compulsory vaccination laws have been in force there for very many years past.

That the board has by its strong advocacy of the effectiveness of vaccination as a protective measure succeeded in inducing more than one-half of the population of Sydney and suburbs to protect themselves in this manner.

That sea quarantine, which is admittedly the most effective form of quarantine possible, has proved itself ineffective in preventing importation of this type of smallpox to Sydney.

Therefore, land quarantine, which is of very little effective value in dealing with large communities, cannot be considered satisfactory or necessary.

That, in conclusion the board is of opinion that the proclamation issued by the Federal Government quarantining Sydney should be withdrawn, as it is unnecessary, and while in existence is injurious in many respects to the State of New South Wales in particular, and to the Commonwealth in general.

It was alleged that after-effects of vaccination was the cause of the death of Mr. Frederick Walter Wippell, at the Lewisham Hospital, on the 2nd instant, and for purposes of general information the Premier called for a report in the matter. The cause of death was certified to as "uraemia, due to chronic Bright's disease," and the Director-General of Public Health has expressed the opinion that there could be no connection between vaccination and chronic Bright's disease.

On 18 September 1913, *The Sydney Morning Herald* reported on the smallpox epidemic that was sweeping the city at the time.

Dr Charles Reid (right) was the Federal Chief Quarantine Officer during the smallpox epidemic. He is pictured here in 1913 with Dr John Fox.

The comparison of quarantine at North Head
with a holiday became a common one

Tents were used to house quarantined passengers during large-scale epidemics when existing accommodation provisions proved insufficient. In this photograph taken in the early 1900s, the tents have been set up in the First Class Precinct.

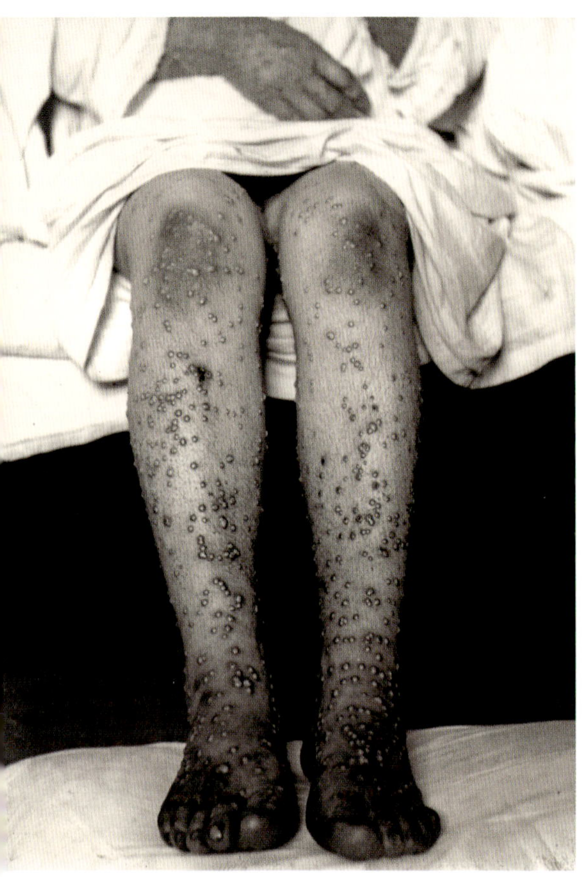

For Thelma Rickett and her family, who lived in the working-class inner-city suburb of Glebe, the experience of quarantine was ironically an enjoyable and novel one. Thelma was six years old when she was sent to the Station during the epidemic, along with her mother and siblings, after the hospitalisation of her father. Apart from a daily check-up by the doctor – searching for the telltale spots – they were left to make their own entertainment, with trips to the beach during the day and singalongs around the piano, playing games and chatting on the verandah at night. For her mother 'it was the cheapest holiday she ever had', with no housework and plenty of good food – and it was probably the closest thing to a family vacation they had ever experienced.

The comparison of quarantine at North Head with a holiday became a common one in the following decades. With advancements in medical treatment and outbreaks quickly brought under control, quarantine was no longer the potential death sentence of the past. Those quarantined at North Head could relax and enjoy the beautiful setting of their detention.

> The brand-new disinfecting section at the Wharf Precinct was up and running by 1919. It included modern autoclaves to thoroughly clean passengers' clothing.

Major Upgrading

The Quarantine Station underwent a major transformation following its transfer to Commonwealth control. In 1911, the new Federal Director for Quarantine, Dr WP Norris, embarked on an overseas study tour to investigate best quarantine practices. In his report tabled in Parliament the following year, Norris advised that although Australia was in regular shipping communication

From Quarantine to Q STATION

with countries where smallpox, yellow fever and bubonic plague epidemics were still rife, its quarantine system was ill equipped to protect the country's inhabitants from imported infectious diseases. He urged that properly equipped quarantine stations be maintained not only in Sydney, but also in Melbourne, Hobart, Brisbane, Adelaide, Fremantle and Albany, with minor stations at five other locations.

Extensive capital works to bring the Station in Sydney up to the necessary standard were carried out between 1912 and 1920. It was transformed into a modern maritime quarantine facility, essentially producing the Station in its current form. For the first time, a building program was implemented as a result of careful planning to meet existing and anticipated needs, rather than as a reaction to shortcomings revealed by quarantine. When the work was completed, the Quarantine Station had state-of-the-art equipment and could accommodate 1208 people, including staff.

⋀ Dr WP Norris was responsible for many innovations at the Quarantine Station, including the building of an Isolation and Observation Block.

NECESSARY CHANGES

In the Wharf Precinct, existing buildings were demolished and a section of the Quarantine Beach shore was reclaimed. Eight buildings equipped with the latest technology were constructed, including a luggage shed, disinfection block, laundry and powerhouse, as well as bathing blocks to be used for the cleaning of passengers and their luggage. Passengers now proceeded to the doctor's room adjoining the luggage shed for a medical examination and classification according to health and passenger-class status before taking a much-needed shower in the new bathing blocks.

The Hospital Precinct was extended with the building of a new ward, a laboratory and a morgue as well as a modern Isolation and Observation Block for any cases of suspected infections. At Collins Flat, the Seamen's Isolation Hospital was also constructed for the treatment of crew members who were infected with general disease.

▼ Like many areas of the Quarantine Station, the revamped Hospital Precinct featured new paling fences to separate it from other precincts. Barbed wire was added for extra security in the Hospital Precinct.

Passengers now proceeded to the doctor's room adjoining the luggage shed for a medical examination and classification according to health and passenger-class status

▲ A separate building that adjoined the new passenger bathing blocks featured several thermo-regulated heating tanks made from corrugated iron.

▼ Third-class passengers had little privacy in their disinfecting showers. The water in which the passengers bathed was mixed with phenol to create an antimicrobial carbolic acid solution.

► With state-of-the-art facilities, the Quarantine Station's modern steam laundry made the chore of cleaning clothes much simpler for long-term detainees.

◄ Constructed in 1912, the narrow-gauge funicular was used to haul suitcases and provisions from the Wharf Precinct to the accommodation and office areas.

◣◥ When they were installed, the autoclaves were considered to be cutting-edge technology. The building was divided into two sections, foul and clean, separated by a wall. Foul materials were wheeled into the chamber, the door was closed and they were disinfected. After treatment, the clean-side doors were opened and the goods taken out and folded.

A further improvement was the installation of a funicular rail system in the Wharf Precinct to transport luggage and stores to the Healthy Ground. It passed from the wharf through the luggage shed and disinfecting chambers, branching around to the bathing blocks before proceeding up the steep sandstone escarpment to the accommodation areas on the Healthy Ground. Passengers had to walk up the steep hill to their allotted quarters, but fortunately the path was punctuated by benches for resting. The infirm were taken up by car.

Pneumonic Influenza Pandemic

The upgrading of the Quarantine Station proved timely, as the new facilities were soon needed to deal with a serious pandemic. In 1918, pneumonic influenza (popularly known as Spanish flu) spread throughout the world. When it reached New Zealand, it was immediately declared a quarantinable disease in Australia. All arriving vessels were subject to quarantine for a mandatory period of up to seven days, and detainees were subjected to a daily 'thermometer parade'.

The passenger liner RMS *Niagara* was the first ship to be quarantined, in October 1918. Large-scale quarantines quickly followed. The troopship *Medic* had 203 cases among the 833 troops and 156 crew members when it arrived in Port Jackson in November 1918. Heading for the Western Front, the troopship had been recalled when peace was declared. When it docked in New Zealand for refuelling on its way back

On Saturday 23 November 1918, *The Sydney Morning Herald* reported on the status of those from the *Medic* who had been quarantined because of influenza.

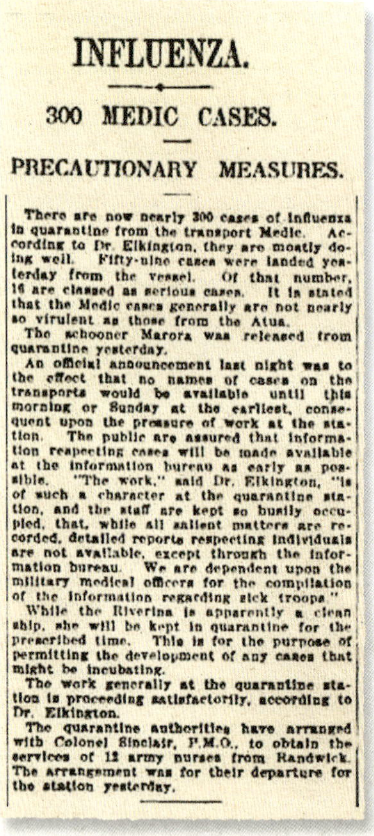

INFLUENZA.

300 MEDIC CASES.

PRECAUTIONARY MEASURES.

There are now nearly 300 cases of influenza in quarantine from the transport Medic. According to Dr. Elkington, they are mostly doing well. Fifty-nine cases were landed yesterday from the vessel. Of that number, 16 are classed as serious cases. It is stated that the Medic cases generally are not nearly so virulent as those from the Atua.

The schooner Marora was released from quarantine yesterday.

An official announcement last night was to the effect that no names of cases on the transports would be available until this morning or Sunday at the earliest, consequent upon the pressure of work at the station. The public are assured that information respecting cases will be made available at the information bureau as early as possible. "The work," said Dr. Elkington, "is of such a character at the quarantine station, and the staff are kept so busily occupied, that, while all salient matters are recorded, detailed reports respecting individuals are not available, except through the information bureau. We are dependent upon the military medical officers for the compilation of the information regarding sick troops."

While the Riverina is apparently a clean ship, she will be kept in quarantine for the prescribed time. This is for the purpose of permitting the development of any cases that might be incubating.

The work generally at the quarantine station is proceeding satisfactorily, according to Dr. Elkington.

The quarantine authorities have arranged with Colonel Sinclair, P.M.O., to obtain the services of 12 army nurses from Randwick. The arrangement was for their departure for the station yesterday.

Carved into a sandstone cliff face near the wharf is an inscription dedicated to the RMS *Niagara*, the first ship to be held in quarantine for influenza in Australia.

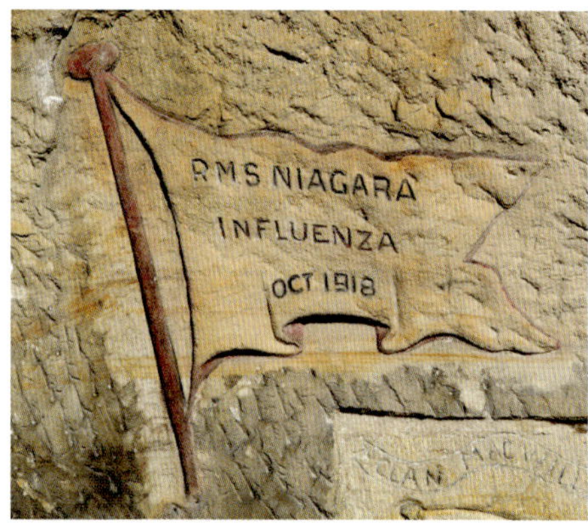

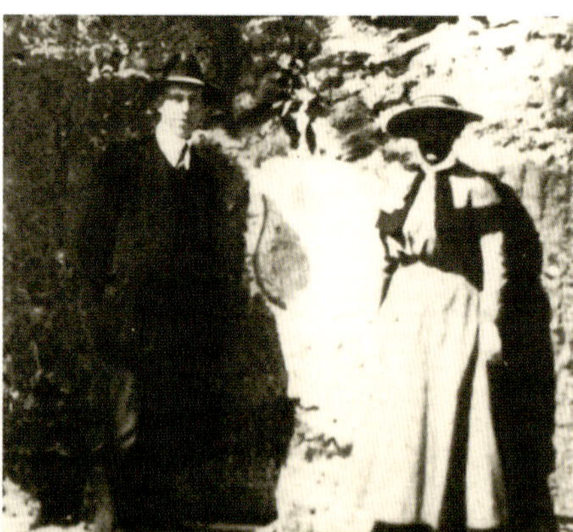

Sister Hargreaves and REA Jeffrey stand either side of an inscription created in their honour by William Kennedy during the quarantine of the RMS *Niagara* in 1918.

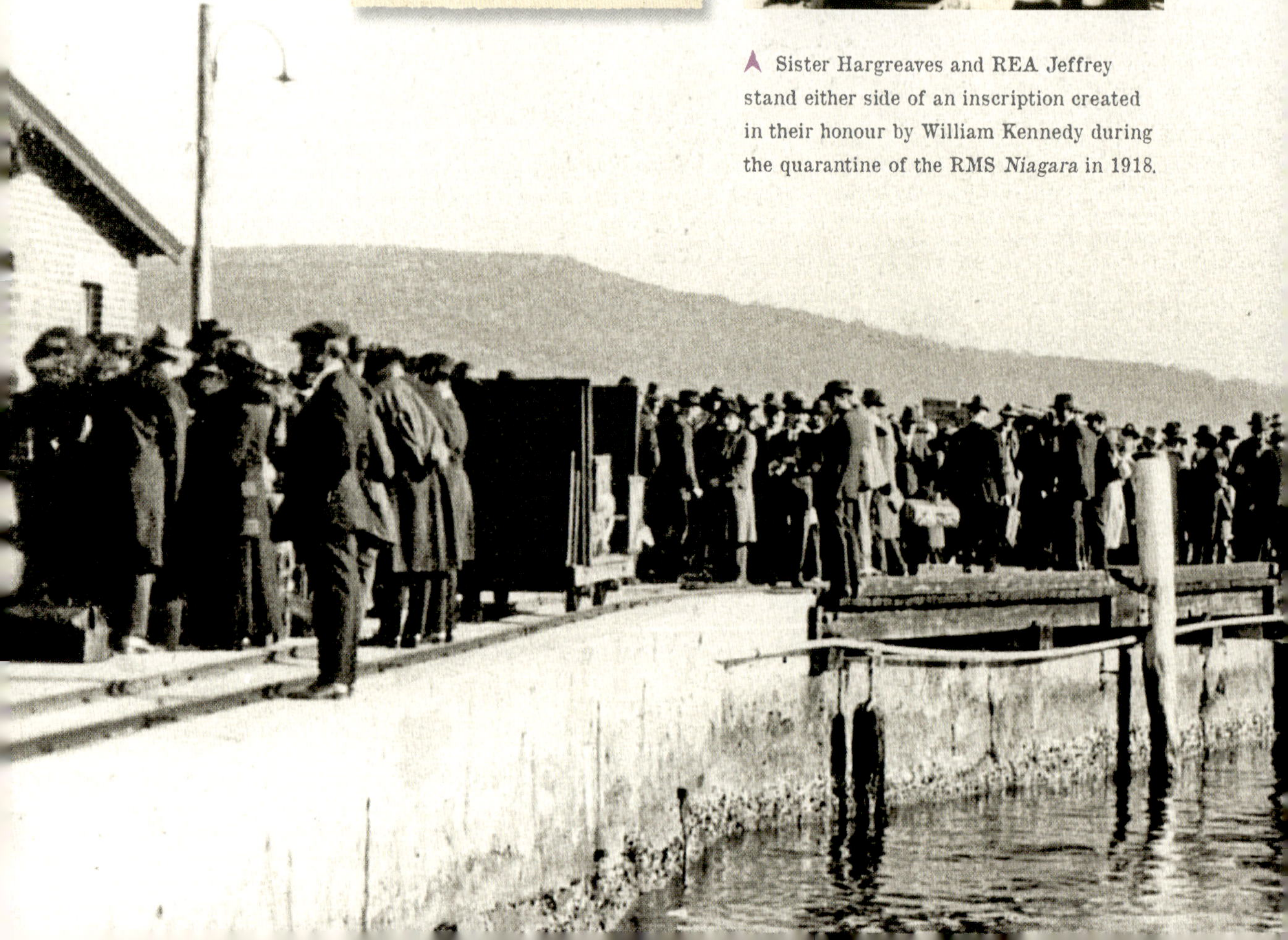

to Sydney, a group of soldiers went ashore. As Alec Dill, a young army sergeant on the *Medic*, recalled years later, the influenza quickly took hold. By the following morning, 'troops' were found unconscious in the scuppers and all over the ship with 'the whole deck turned into a hospital'.

Nineteen-year-old Harry Hansell was another soldier on the *Medic* who contracted influenza during the voyage back to Sydney. Among those still able to talk when the troops were landed at the Station, he recalls first undergoing a steam disinfection procedure in a makeshift inhalation chamber with bench seating for about 20 people set up on the ship's deck. As the source of the influenza was understood to be bacteria in the lungs rather than a virus, the quarantined were required to inhale a solution containing zinc sulphate to disinfect both the throat and air passages. Two inhalation chambers were installed in the disinfecting block in the Wharf Precinct in 1919 for this procedure.

Passengers from the RMS *Niagara*, now free of influenza, board the *Kookaburra*, which would take them from the Quarantine Station to Sydney – their original destination.

DEATH AND DILEMMA

Between November 1918 and March 1919, a total of 110 ships carrying over 12,000 people were quarantined in Port Jackson. On one occasion as many as 13 ships were moored in Spring Cove. Fifteen ships in total had infected people aboard, with 70 people dying at the Quarantine Station of influenza, including 14 servicemen, two army nurses, nine Italian reservists and one member of quarantine staff. The remaining casualties were mostly Fijian and Pacific Islander passengers and crew.

One of the nurses to die was 27-year-old Annie Egan. Despite being inoculated against influenza, she fell ill in November 1918 while caring for troops from the *Medic*, just days after she had arrived. As her condition deteriorated, Nurse Egan asked for a Catholic priest to administer the last sacraments. Her request was denied. The long-standing practice of allowing clergymen to visit the Station during quarantine had been stopped when

A busy period at the Quarantine Station ended in March 1919. Thousands of men and women from all walks of life found themselves in quarantine – some sick enough to require hospital treatment.

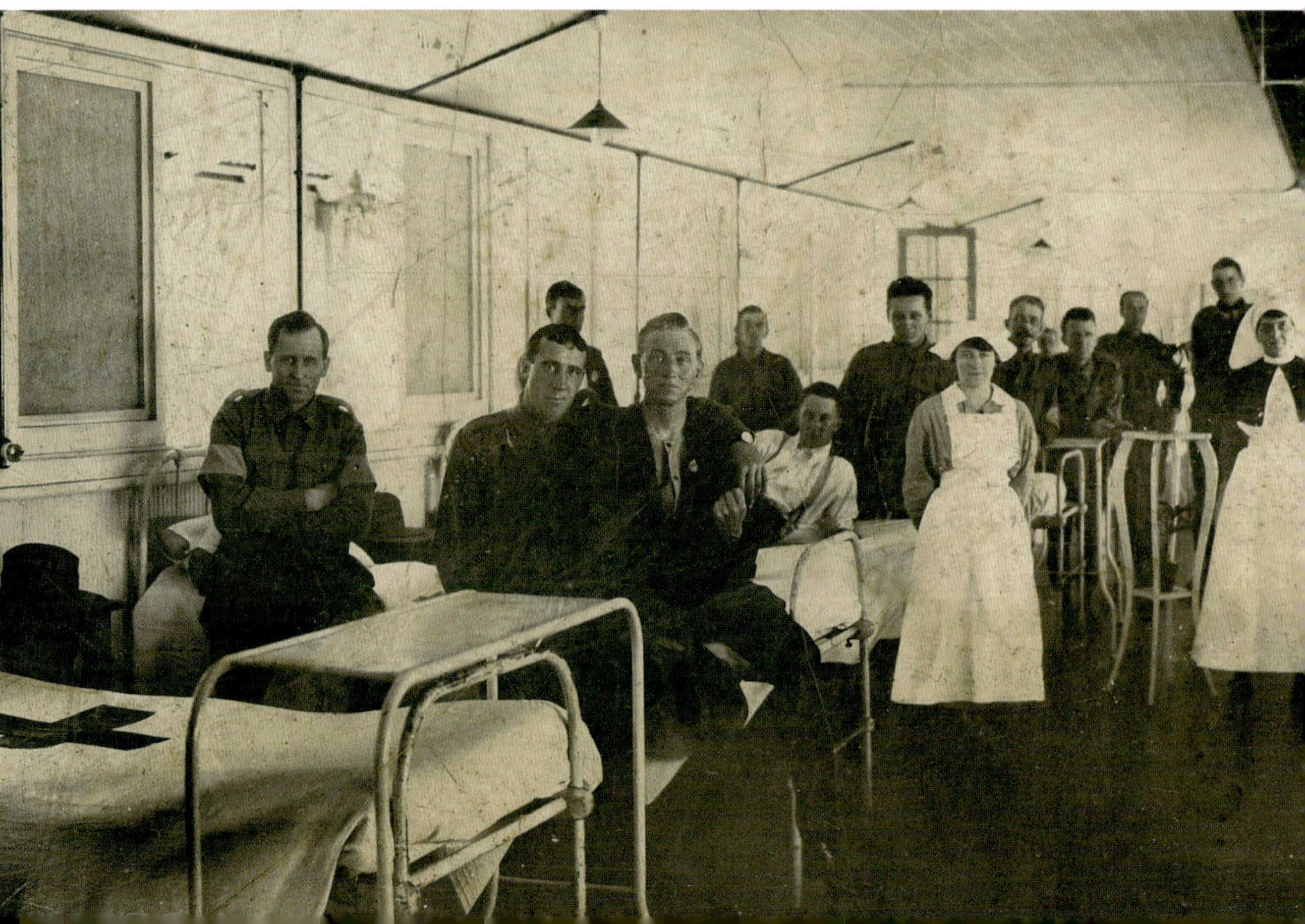

the Commonwealth Government took over control because of the potential risk of reviving infection.

The story of Nurse Egan's plight reached the newspapers and caused a public furore. A high-profile campaign by the Catholic Church (led by Archbishop Michael Kelly) for the policy to be reversed saw the government finally capitulate on 10 December. But it was too late for Annie Egan, who had died on 3 December. Another army nurse, Elizabeth McGregor, fell victim to influenza two days later. They were both buried with full military honours, their coffins covered by wreaths made by quarantined servicemen from wild flowers growing at the Station.

▲ Nearly half of all the ships that were quarantined over the entire time the Station was in operation were detained during the summer of 1918–19 as a result of the influenza pandemic.

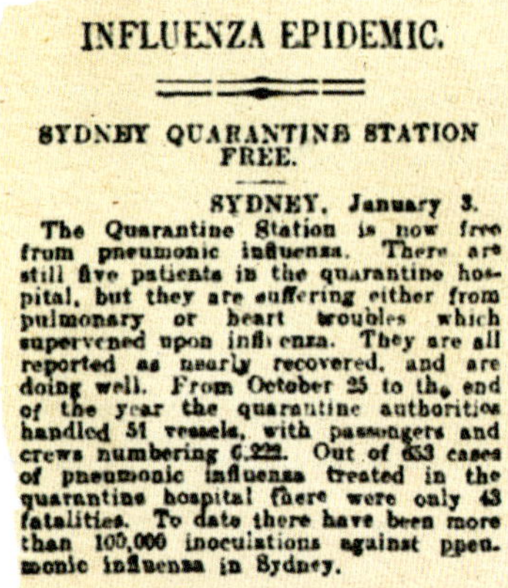

▲ On 4 January 1919, Hobart's *The Mercury* newspaper reported that the Quarantine Station was free of influenza; this news had come from Sydney a day earlier. It soon became obvious, however, that the virus had actually escaped quarantine and was spreading through Sydney.

➤ People linger on a verandah in the First Class Precinct in 1918 during their quarantine for influenza. Boredom was a constant issue, as entertainment options were not provided by quarantine officials.

In January 1919, influenza broke through the quarantine barrier and infected Sydney residents. Three weeks earlier *The Sydney Morning Herald* newspaper had prematurely declared that all was under control, reporting that thanks to the 'ceaseless and heroic' battle in the past 10 weeks during which 6222 people had been quarantined from 51 ships, the Station had been free of disease for five days.

Family members were prohibited from seeing their quarantined relatives and had to rely on lists published daily in the newspapers describing the condition of the patients in the Station's hospital. Relatives gathered outside the Station in the vain hope of a glimpse or news of loved ones.

TROOP UNREST

With the Station unable to cope with the swelling numbers of residents, quarantined troops cleared bush areas for the erection of tent accommodation. By early January 1919, there were some 2500 people quarantined at the Station, and lockdown was enforced by a large contingent of troops who guarded the entrance and patrolled the grounds. The Sydney Police Force was also sent to the Station to maintain order, including a night launch patrol of Spring Cove.

Resenting their detainment and anxious to get home, many of the servicemen were extremely bored and restless. Aside from the spectacular views, Harry Hansell also remembers the Quarantine Station as a 'windswept, desolate place' with little to do to pass the time. Letters were the only form of contact with the outside world. Minor skirmishes among the soldiers were not uncommon.

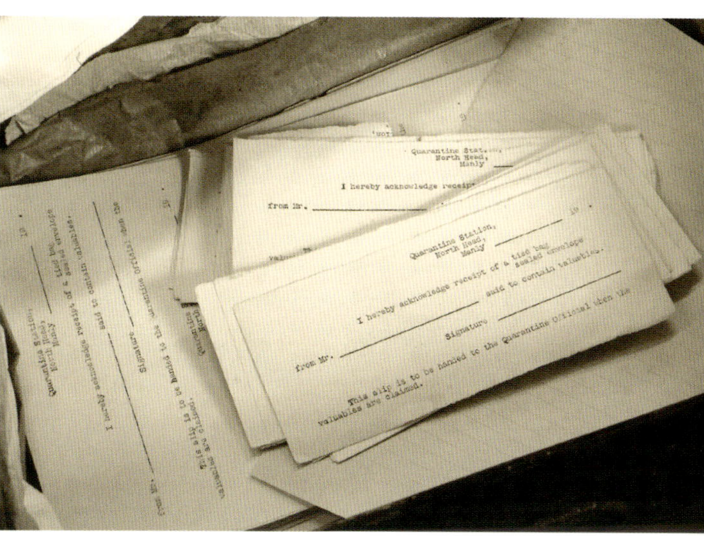

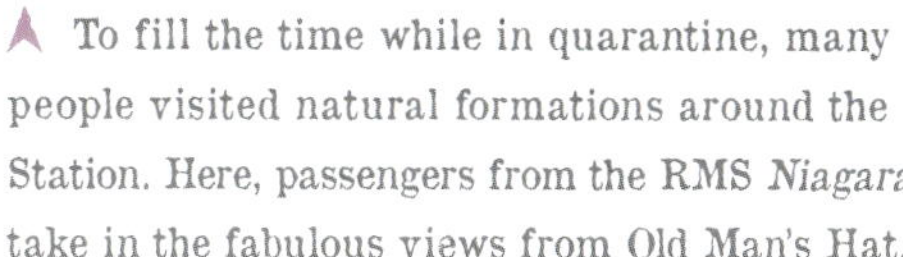

▲ To fill the time while in quarantine, many people visited natural formations around the Station. Here, passengers from the RMS *Niagara* take in the fabulous views from Old Man's Hat.

▲ When the Quarantine Station was crowded, it was difficult to keep track of all the valuables brought into the Station by passengers. These receipts were used to simplify the process.

Family members were prohibited from seeing their quarantined relatives and had to rely on lists published daily in the newspapers describing the condition of the patients

To keep all the children entertained while in quarantine, the adults arranged fun games and races. Here, children are running down Main Axial Street in the First Class Precinct.

Necessity became the mother of invention at the Station. Looking for something to help children pass the time, someone created a unique race using buckets and potatoes.

Reflecting a tradition that is still observed in modern backyards across Australia, a rubbish bin was used as a makeshift wicket in a game of cricket at the Quarantine Station.

Downturn in Maritime Quarantine

Although the Station was rated among the best quarantine facilities in the world, from the 1920s the need for human quarantine at the Station declined. The effectiveness of public health measures and increased medical knowledge, together with the impact of a Federal quarantine system, ensured that the influenza pandemic was the last serious quarantine event. There were only 55 ships quarantined from 1921 to 1975, and two deaths at the Station after 1919: a crew member from tuberculosis in 1925, and a passenger from liver disease in 1962.

Quarantine became an entirely different experience. There were plenty of social and recreational options, including tennis and quoits, swimming at the beach, fishing, dances and concerts. Boredom rather than serious illness became the most debilitating aspect of detention. When the passenger liner *Aorangi* was quarantined during February 1930 because a crew member was suspected of having smallpox, there was never any great risk to the health of passengers. Archibald Howie, who was in his early twenties and travelling first class on his return from New Zealand, recalled, 'it was a lovely place to spend a holiday, provided you didn't mind the fact that you were stuck here'. Although passengers were still segregated along passenger-class lines, he was not sure what the difference was, as 'none of it was exactly luxurious' and most of the buildings were 'pretty dingy'. The bedrooms, for example, had uncomfortable iron beds and bare wooden floors.

A group of women enjoy Quarantine Beach in 1926. Taking in the healthful sea breezes and dipping one's toes in the cool water was a very agreeable way to spend the day.

Boredom rather than serious illness became the most debilitating aspect of detention

Photographed in c. 1920, these women have just emerged from a disinfecting shower. All passengers and crew were required to undertake a thorough decontamination shower on landing.

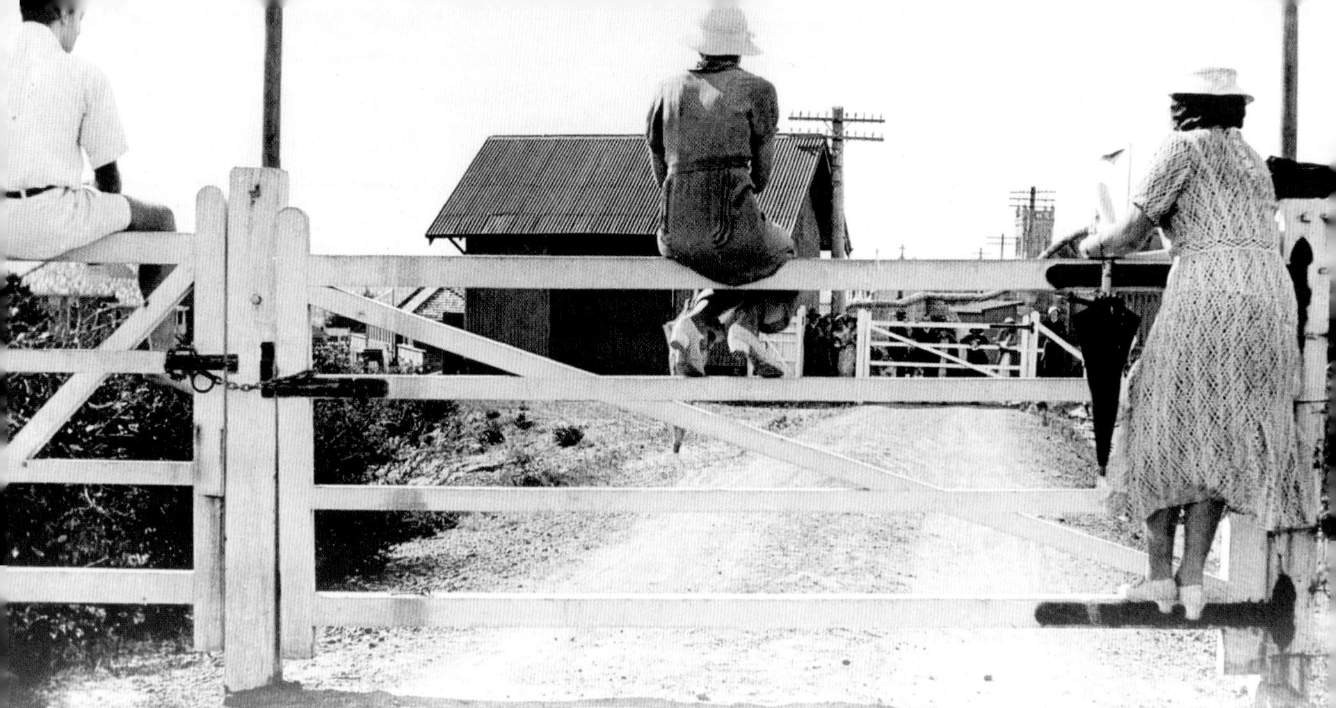

The *Aorangi* was again quarantined in January 1935 for just under three weeks. Passengers described their stay as a fun experience, with a holiday atmosphere on the Station. According to passenger Elaine Reid, once the bad news of the quarantine was announced, 'we got over our shock and made the most of our stay there'. She recalls most of the passengers being 'on the go all the time', playing tennis and swimming during the day, with dancing and other organised activities at night. She spent every day at Store Beach, and on her son's birthday, 'everybody rallied around and went through their luggage to find presents for him'.

▲ **Family and friends who visited quarantined passengers from the *Aorangi* were forced to communicate with their loved ones by shouting from a gate some 30 metres away.**

➤ **Following their release from quarantine, cheerful and relaxed passengers from the *Aorangi* waited patiently at Quarantine Wharf for a ferry to take them to Sydney.**

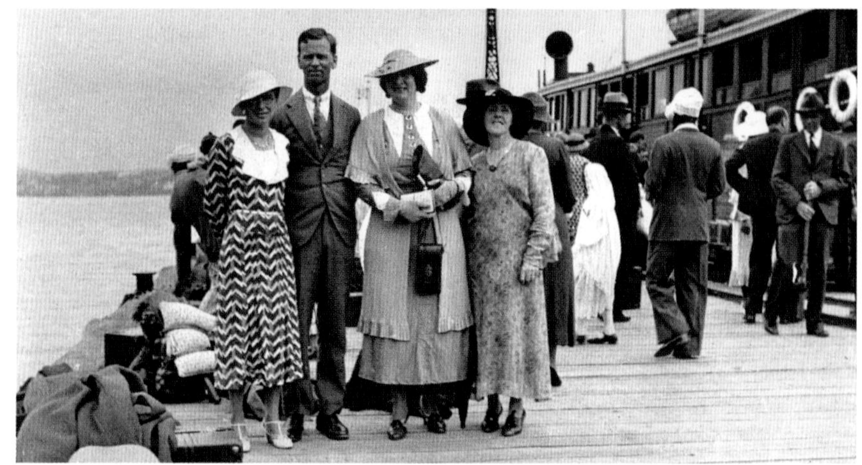

▲ When they weren't busy with detainees, Quarantine Station employees were able to enjoy the site's views and natural facilities, such as Store Beach, at their leisure.

▼ Children quarantined in the mid-1930s made the most of the available space within the First Class Precinct by holding boisterous three-legged races.

► In the 1930s, the Station's beaches were the one place where a passenger's class was irrelevant. Here, travellers from the *Aorangi* form a human pyramid on Store Beach.

◄ Even during the mid-1930s, quarantine was highly regimented. There was a strict daily routine that began with a complete morning medical examination, and a lights-out curfew was enforced at night.

 From Quarantine to ʠSTATION

The Postwar Years

During World War II, the Quarantine Station was primarily used for military-related purposes. The buildings were run down and in desperate need of repair by the war's end, but building material shortages and the low demand for quarantine created very little incentive for improvement. Between 1950 and 1973, only 12 ships were quarantined. This reflected both marked advances in medical science – especially the treatment and prevention of infection with antibiotics and immunisation – and the emergence of air travel as a form of mass transport. All passengers arriving at ports of entry in Sydney (including Kingsford Smith Airport at Mascot) without the required current smallpox vaccination certificates, as well as inoculation for cholera and yellow fever, were automatically subject to quarantine.

The standard of accommodation was totally unsatisfactory, with worn and old-fashioned furniture, unlined walls, iron beds with too-thin mattresses, flaking paint, chipped crockery and phones that did not work. But complaints from airline officials about the inadequacy of the facility, following the quarantine of aircraft passengers from three separate international flights in February and March 1951, were largely ignored.

▲ John MacMahon, the son of one of the Quarantine Station's general labourers, was photographed playing happily in his billycart in front of the staff cottages in 1948.

◄ Taken in the 1940s, this black-and-white aerial photograph reveals the layout of the Quarantine Station's buildings during and just after World War II.

◄ Doctors at the international terminal of Kingsford Smith Airport in Sydney check the paperwork of incoming passengers to ensure that they have received all the required inoculations.

Much of the work at the Quarantine Station during the 1950s involved the disinfecting of luggage belonging to the enormous wave of migrants from Europe. Under the Federal Government's postwar immigration policy, large numbers of southern Europeans began arriving in Australia from rural areas where foot-and-mouth disease was still running wild. Because foot-and-mouth disease was last seen in Australia in 1872 – and the disease has a long incubation period – strict quarantine measures were put in place to minimise the risk of the disease being reintroduced. On arrival, European migrants from rural areas who had travelled to Australia by air were taken to the Quarantine Station for disinfection of their clothing, footwear and other belongings; the clothing worn at the time of arrival (except underwear) was put through the autoclaves for disinfection.

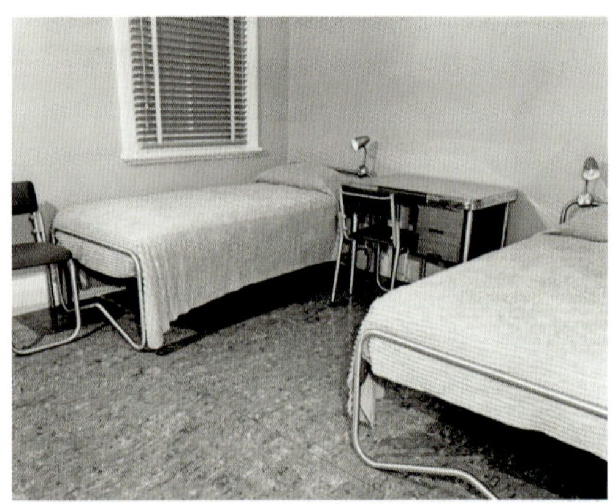

A modernisation program to bring the Station up to a standard acceptable to airline passengers was finally carried out in the late 1950s. The removal of 11 buildings reduced the accommodation capacity to 250 people. Following the Station's improvement, there was only one large quarantine event – 29 international aircraft passengers suspected of having cholera in 1972. In 1973, the tanker *Sakaki Maru* became the last ship to be quarantined; it was held for a short period after a suspected smallpox case, although the crew did not disembark. The only people quarantined at the Station after this were airline passengers arriving without adequate vaccination certificates. In 1975, for example, this totalled 78 persons.

Newly arrived migrant workers from Europe and their personal baggage were put through stringent decontamination processes so that foot-and-mouth disease did not re-enter Australia.

In the 1950s, imported coir matting and other goods that may have come into contact with infectious disease were disinfected in the Station's large English-made autoclaves.

Most of the Second Cemetery's gravestones were replaced with brass grave markers on posts in the 1950s. Unfortunately, due to the value of brass, these were stolen over the following years.

Emergency Relief

By the early 1970s, the Station's staff was reduced to eight. As quarantine often involved only one or two people, it was an expensive system, although its large accommodation capacity did prove useful as an emergency facility. After Cyclone Tracy devastated Darwin on Christmas Day in 1974, it was used to house 213 evacuees. In April the following year, 115 of 215 Vietnamese orphans, aged between three months and 10 years and evacuated by the Federal Government shortly before the fall of Saigon, were housed there before being united with their adoptive parents.

> After Cyclone Tracy devastated Darwin on Christmas Day in 1974, [the Quarantine Station] was used to house 213 evacuees

Closure of the Quarantine Station

By the late 1970s, the eradication of smallpox and the dramatic advances in the control of human disease – as well as changing patterns of travel and trade – required a major change in the approach to human quarantine. New and acutely infectious diseases that could not be properly treated in traditional quarantine stations (notably viral haeomorrhagic fevers such as Lassa fever and Marburg virus disease) began to appear. In 1977, the Federal Government decided to establish a high-security unit at the Fairfield Infectious Diseases Hospital in Melbourne. Significant changes also occurred in the area of animal and plant quarantine, as the natural barrier afforded by Australia's isolation was eroded by more rapid transport.

From Quarantine to ꓢTATION

Australia's quarantine stations were closed in the following years, with Sydney being the last, in 1984. By that time, at least 580 vessels and more than 13,000 people had been quarantined at the Station, and an estimated 572 unfortunate people never got to leave – they are buried in the three cemeteries located within the grounds. The land on which the Station was built reverted to State ownership on 16 March 1984 in accordance with the terms of the original transfer agreement of 1911. By then, the site reserved for quarantine purposes had been reduced to just 27 hectares. It became part of the Sydney Harbour National Park under the management of the New South Wales National Parks and Wildlife Service.

Every stage of the Quarantine Station's use and development mirrors the rapid changes that occurred in Australian society from the time of British settlement. From a purely contemporary perspective, it may seem that it was a cruel and barbaric place in those early years, but it was merely a microcosm of the wider community. It is easy to forget that a public health system did not emerge until the latter part of the nineteenth century. That the Station became something akin to a holiday camp is testament to the rapid development and impact of modern medicine in the following century. The Station entered yet another phase in its history when it closed, similarly reflecting shifts in community thinking. A source of great contention in the expanding Manly community from the 1880s, plans for its future conservation were to be contested some 100 years later.

⌃ Jane Aberdeen is one of the people still buried at the Station. She arrived on the *Lady MacNaghton* in February 1837 and died from typhus fever, aged just 17 months.

⪢ In April 1975, local children presented a box of toys, nappies and other gifts to a staff member for the Vietnamese orphans staying at the Station.

⌄ Now part of Sydney Harbour National Park, the Quarantine Station site is a peaceful place where you can discover an incredible slice of Australia's history.

QUARANTINE
VERBODEN
ZONE DE QUARANTAINE
L'ENTRÉE INTERDIT
Snugglers
nappy and waterproof
pants in one
KALEIDOSCOPE

QUARANTINE AREA
TRESPASSERS PROSECUTED
QUARANTINE

⋀ This **SS** *Chingtu* inscription is located at Old Man's Hat, a large rock formation on the southern coast of North Head. Despite being exposed to the elements for over 100 years, the writing is still visible.

➤ The weather wears away the soft sandstone at North Head, and large chunks often come tumbling down. Fortunately, in this case most of the inscriptions carved into the sandstone survived the fall.

Chapter 4

Stories from the Sandstone

Along the cliff face at North Head, on a low sheltered rock face, someone has etched a pair of concentric circles. These appear to form the shape of a belt, complete with a buckle and tightening holes. Emerging from either side of the belt is another carved image – a rope with an anchor tied to one end. Carefully spaced within the belt are the words 'VICTORIAN . NAVAL . CONTINGENT'. Inside the inner circle, topped by a six-pointed star, the inscription reads 'S.S. CHINGTU / MAY / 1901'. This carving required careful planning and considerable effort, so who made it? By combining both archaeological and historical research, this and other stories from the sandstone are emerging from the Quarantine Station's complex past.

The Tale of the SS *Chingtu*

The China Navigation Company steamship *Chingtu* was quarantined in Sydney on 25 April 1901, because a case of smallpox was detected on board between Hong Kong and Thursday Island. Arriving from China, the ship brought home sailors and soldiers who had volunteered to fight against militant societies in the anti-Western uprising known as the Boxer Rebellion.

Having departed in 1900 as colonials with the New South Wales and Victorian Naval Contingents, these men returned as Australian citizens. Their time in China had spanned not only the proclamation of the Commonwealth of Australia on 1 January 1901, but also the death of Britain's Queen Victoria just three weeks later. These events opened a new century in which Australia's place in the world – and especially its connections with Pacific Ocean neighbours – would change dramatically.

⌃ The Victorian Naval Contingent embarked at Port Melbourne. Due to smallpox, some of these men were detained at the Quarantine Station on their return from China to Australia.

⌄ This evocative 1901 watercolour by John Downs Castle (1858–1928) shows the SS *Chingtu* cutting through the waves on its way to Sydney from China's Boxer Rebellion.

Arthur Livingstone was among the many men from the SS *Chingtu* who were put ashore at North Head. After marvelling at the views of Sydney Harbour, he admired the Quarantine Station's impressive accommodation facilities. He had, after all, spent the previous eight months sleeping in tents, stables and hammocks. Venturing out for a stroll around the cliffs of North Head, Livingstone found the names of numerous ships and their company flags carved into the sandstone, including several that were 'painted in all different colours … & look very well'. Reading these inscriptions, he noted that the SS *Chingtu* had already been quarantined twice before; only one of these engravings can now be located.

By the time they were released from quarantine in late May 1901, Livingstone's comrades from the Victorian Naval Contingent had added their own elaborate carving to this outdoor gallery. Meanwhile, Charles Harvey – a Victorian from the SS *Chingtu* – chose the prominent wall of inscriptions at the Quarantine Station's wharf area to carve his own name and rank – 'AB2', for able-bodied seaman. Returning home to Port Melbourne, Harvey sadly died in 1907 after being run over by a train, apparently while walking home drunk.

One soldier, however, never left North Head. Although two smallpox patients from the SS *Chingtu* recovered, a Sydney man serving in the New South Wales Marine Light Infantry was less fortunate. Several weeks into the quarantine, Charles Walter Smart developed the characteristic rash and died of smallpox on 20 May. Rather than receiving full military honours, he was hurriedly buried in the dark of night at the Quarantine Station's Third Cemetery. Paid for by former comrades, his expensive headstone still stands there, facing South Head and the surging Pacific Ocean.

⋀ Charles Harvey spent a considerable amount of time and effort inscribing his name and rank into the sandstone near the Spring Cove wharf.

⋀⋀ In August 1893, the SS *Chingtu* was quarantined because a crew member came down with smallpox. The inscription marking that event is attributed to engineer Mat Warton.

➤➤ Overgrown with shrubs and grasses, the Quarantine Station's Third Cemetery – the last resting place of Charles Walter Smart – now offers spectacular views of Sydney.

Carving Out a Partnership

These episodes from the 1901 quarantine of the SS *Chingtu* sit among the thousands that can be located in the words and shapes carved across North Head. It was in order to draw out such stories that a partnership was formed between Q Station and The University of Sydney in 2011. Having spent decades investigating Indigenous archaeology – including depictions of contact with Macassan and European ships – archaeologist Dr Annie Clarke found herself drawn to these intriguing inscriptions across North Head. She soon crossed paths with a medical historian, Professor Alison Bashford, who not only had an established reputation as a scholar of quarantine, but was also a local resident who often explored this sandstone headland.

Dr Clarke and Professor Bashford approached The Mawland Group with a proposal for a collaborative research project based around Q Station's historic inscriptions. The enthusiastic response from The Mawland Group led to a joint application to the Commonwealth Government for a prestigious Australian Research Council grant to investigate the archaeology and history of the site. After a rigorous and competitive review process, this proposal was awarded a substantial grant in 2012. As a result of this three-way linkage between The Mawland Group, The University of Sydney and the Australian Government, the intriguing 'Stories from the Sandstone' project commenced in January 2013 and ran until December 2015.

The visit of the SS *Tsinan* – whose crew and passengers spent Christmas 1905 in quarantine due to a smallpox outbreak – is just one of the tales linked to inscriptions at North Head.

JUST THREE LETTERS?

Often overlooked in favour of the more colourful carvings nearby, the inscription commemorating the quarantine of the SS *St Albans* in February 1917 features several overlapping stories. Signed only by 'S A H', detailed research starting with the ship's crew list revealed that the author was Samuel Alfred ('Alf') Hollingsworth, son of an Irish cow-keeper, who made a career of the sea. Alongside the ship's mostly Chinese crew and passengers, Alf was quarantined during the middle of World War I when smallpox was detected on the ship. After he left his brief memorial to their time at North Head, an educated Chinese passenger – or possibly a highly ranked crewman – penned the skilled Chinese calligraphy that sits inside the same panel. Its meaning has been translated to say: 'Erected in the sixth year of the [Chinese] Republic, first month, twenty-fifth day, to commemorate St Albans'. Hidden for many years underneath layers of whitewash, this anonymous Chinese text is re-emerging as the top coat wears away.

➤ Dinah and Alfred ('Alf') Hollingsworth are pictured here in 1954, almost 40 years after Alf left his mark at the Quarantine Station during his seafaring days.

With both English and Chinese lettering, the SS *St Albans* inscription reflects the multicultural nature of some ships' crews in the early twentieth century.

THREEFOLD PROJECT OBJECTIVES

Firstly, there are at least 1500 historic inscriptions carved, painted or cemented into the landscape right across North Head. Their abundance makes this a unique heritage site of global importance. However, their location – etched into soft stone and exposed to all manner of environmental factors – means that each one of these inscriptions will gradually disappear. Therefore, the archaeology team led by Dr Clarke and colleague Dr Ursula Frederick located and documented as many inscriptions as possible to create a permanent record of this vanishing cultural resource.

> Etched into soft stone and exposed to all manner of environmental factors … each one of these inscriptions will gradually disappear

AORANGI
1930
1935

AORANGI
1930
1935

▲ Not surprisingly, Charles Walter Smart's white headstone is a little weathered after spending more than a century standing quiet sentinel over his lonely grave in the Quarantine Station's Third Cemetery.

➤ Dr Annie Clarke brings the 'Stories from the Sandstone' to life for a keen tour group. In retelling the tales, Dr Clarke ensures that modern visitors fully appreciate the unique human history of the Quarantine Station.

Secondly, although it's impossible to trace the circumstances behind the creation of each inscription, many carvings have a story to tell. Sometimes – as with the SS *Chingtu* inscriptions and Charles Walter Smart's headstone – historical research draws together multiple locations into a single historical moment. From such moments, larger histories can be explored – the growth of Sydney, the impact of epidemics, the experience of quarantine, its links to immigration and racial discrimination, and the place held by Australia in a globe crisscrossed by maritime trade. Drawing these unique connections out of the historical record was the task of Professor Bashford and fellow historian Dr Peter Hobbins.

Thirdly, the archaeological and historical research for the 'Stories from the Sandstone' project has contributed directly to understanding the ongoing heritage of Sydney's Quarantine Station. Information documented throughout the project was integrated into educational programs, guided tours, interpretive signs, the museum collection, conservation policies – even maintenance and gardening work. A database of the inscriptions and related historical information was created as a resource for visitors and family historians, while presentations and publications by project members promoted Q Station's unique heritage value to global audiences.

◄ Even those arriving by air were subject to quarantine occasionally, and they, like ships' passengers before them, left reminders of their presence in the soft sandstone.

CAGING THE SPEEDBIRD

The peak years of activity at the Quarantine Station had long passed by the late 1930s, when regular airline flights to Australia were established. The last major ocean liner quarantine occurred in 1949, so there was a flurry of activity in February 1951 when buses arrived from Sydney airport bearing the crew and passengers from two airliners. The first, flying from London, was operated by the British Overseas Airways Corporation (BOAC), while the second was a Dutch aircraft flown by KLM. Both had been found in Darwin to be carrying passengers suffering from influenza, which at the time was rapidly spreading across Europe. Among those affected was a 21-year-old Thai student, Achar Romyanandana, who was coming

▶ Like all 'alien residents' of Australia in the 1950s, Achar Romyanandana had to complete a registration form before arrival in the country.

to Australia to undertake a three-year course at Brisbane Agricultural College. Although they were held in separate parts of the station, most of the passengers enjoyed the time they spent in quarantine, especially the Dutch, who yelled to a reporter in a rowboat offshore: 'This is paradise; we never want to leave here.' One memento of this brief visit was the complex inscription that records not only the date and the name of the Royal Mail Aircraft *Beaufort*, registered G-ALAN, but also the initials of BOAC and the airline's famous 'Speedbird' logo.

Connecting Inscriptions

Unfortunately, what made North Head the ideal spot for the creation of inscriptions is also why these precious carvings are so endangered – the soft Hawkesbury sandstone and its exposed location. The latter was, of course, why the headland was chosen as the site for the Quarantine Station: isolated from the growing township of Sydney, it offered a safe harbour for incoming vessels, fresh water and healthy breezes.

By the time that the ship *Canton* was quarantined in 1835, many visitors – perhaps inspired by existing Aboriginal rock art in the area – had already established that North Head's sandstone was the perfect medium for creating enduring markers of their presence. Subsequently, over 1000 quarantine detainees followed their lead, leaving anything from a single letter to complicated memorials that include frames, pictures, lists of names and patches of colour. The archaeologists worked hard to make detailed notes, draw careful sketches and create a definitive photographic record of what remains of each identifiable inscription.

VARIED STONEWORK

After spending months carefully inspecting and documenting the many inscriptions across North Head, the archaeologists developed a fine appreciation for its variations. Over millions of years, Sydney's sandstone was laid down in beds that alternate from hard and dense to soft and powdery. The many different stonemasons who came into quarantine in the nineteenth century chose their stone carefully – it is often their large, elaborate and well-sited carvings that survive the best. Less trained eyes may have selected stone that was easier to work – but it was also more prone to damage and erosion. In some cases, it's clear that the damage occurred while carving was still underway.

Historians and archaeologists worked closely together at the Quarantine Station to unravel the meaning behind both simple and complicated text and pictorial inscriptions.

Equally important was the time put in to each project: inscriptions with deep incisions and the addition of paint or pitch have generally endured better than those with shallow scratches and sloppy brushwork. Ironically, the inscriptions most at risk now at Q Station are those from the 1960s and 1970s, when the building known as A20 was used not for quarantine, but to detain stowaways and other foreign nationals awaiting deportation. Written in pencil or pen on the painted interior walls, these recent inscriptions are fading, flaking and peeling away at an alarming rate.

◄▲ Even before the inscription dedicated to the SS *Roggeveen* was conserved (right), the black pitch outline of the circle was still clearly visible, as was most of the deeply carved ship's name.

C NEUMANN
JOHN
ALICE OLIVER
GEORGE
JULY
C RIDDELL
M TAYLOR
JRB

HISTORY AT RISK

What is clear from comparing Q Station's inscriptions with historical photographs, or even with archaeological recordings made since the 1980s, is that all are at risk. Sandstone is particularly vulnerable to damage by water. While rain and run-off dissolve the stone, the greatest risk is penetration by moist sea air laden with salt. Even if the water moves out of the stone, the salt remains to weaken its structure, leading to crumbling or splitting. Being surrounded by the ocean, there is little that can be done to halt this process. Erosion of the inscriptions is further accelerated by wind, pollution, accidental or wilful damage and the creeping roots of trees, shrubs, mosses and lichens. As plants and soil constantly attempt to reclaim the site, even quite large and elaborately carved boulders can quickly vanish under vigorous bush regrowth. Some have been lost within a decade.

The task before the archaeologists was therefore not just to document the known inscriptions, but to locate again those that had faded from sight – and from memory – over 10, 50 or even 150 years. It was an enormous task, given that the Quarantine Station once occupied almost all of North Head. In addition to the prominent wall of carvings at the wharf area, inscriptions are scattered alongside buildings and roads throughout Q Station. But they can also be found around the flagpole at Cannae Point – the small 'island' beyond the wharf area – as well as one cove away at Store Beach, where supplies for the station were once dropped. A large number are hidden under scrub on the flat and fragile cliff face beyond Q Station known as Old Man's Hat, where Arthur Livingstone found the memorials to the SS *Chingtu* over a century ago. Another 100 inscriptions are located further away at a remote obelisk, one of the earliest European structures on North Head, which dates back as far as 1837.

◄ Lichen is slowly growing over and irreparably damaging the RMS *Australia* inscription. This passenger ship was quarantined in March 1898 for smallpox.

⋀ Archaeologists Iain Johnston and Dr Ursula Frederick struggle to read the words of the lichen-covered inscription marking the quarantine of the SS *Mariposa* in February 1888.

◄ The crowded cluster of inscriptions at Old Man's Hat is starting to fade away. Only the deepest carvings are still legible, but even those will eventually deteriorate over time.

SS S'ALBANS
FEB 1917
SAH
紀　念
廿六中
五年華
元共
月和
生了路林

S NIAGARA
FLUENZA
OCT 1918
CLAN MACWILLIAM
S.S. ROGGEVEEN
BATAVIA
JAN. 1920

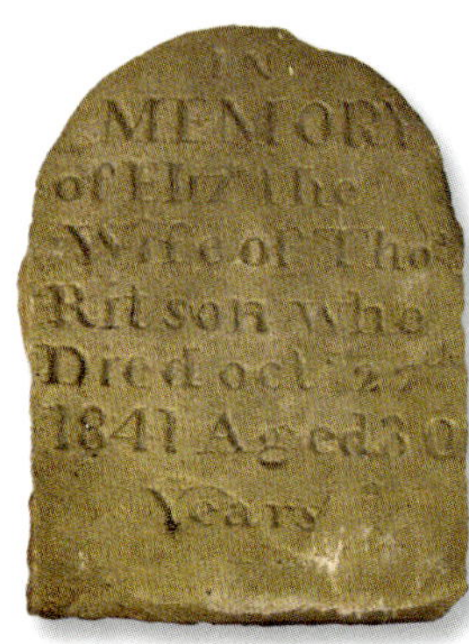

Finally, there are the many poignant gravestones that can be found in Q Station's museum collection, as well as those still in place at the Former Second and Third Cemeteries. The latter is where Charles Walter Smart still rests – even if the headstone incorrectly notes his name as 'W.C. Smart'. This is not unusual – often the historical records and archaeological evidence don't neatly match up.

Translating the Past for the Present

So how does the sandstone reveal its stories? Via scrutiny of the archaeological recordings and searching far and wide through collections of historical documents. This variety of sources is why it remains so important for historians and archaeologists to work as a team.

In contrast to documentary records, which are often based on varying first-person testimonies, archaeological analysis provides more concrete information. It offers insights into changing stylistic and mark-making conventions, the tools and materials that people had at their disposal, and the time and thought put into marking their presence. Archaeologists also seek to explain the shifting distribution of text and images, both within individual engravings and across the landscape as a whole. By discerning patterns in what's present and absent from the inscriptions, archaeological research can contribute knowledge about the way that human attributes such as ethnicity, social class and gender were viewed and 'pictured' in the past.

With so many possibilities to begin with, only a sample of the inscriptions could be researched in detail. These were the 'stories from the sandstone' fleshed out by historical research (see pages 89, 93 and 102–3 for three of the stories). Who carved these messages? Why? How long were they detained at North Head? Who arrived alongside them? Was their stay dull, pleasant, painful or touched by bereavement? What led them to leave their homes for Sydney? What happened after they arrived and settled? What other marks did they leave on Sydney, New South Wales or Australia? How can their passage through the Quarantine Station – as individuals or as groups – help us better understand the wider past?

Many inscriptions are too brief or too damaged to provide meaningful clues as to their origin. How do we know who is represented by the stylised monogram 'JAB', or by the few letters remaining when a large piece of carved cliff face has crumbled away? Who was the 'I' who scratched 'I WAS HERE' next to a carefully carved figure of a man in uniform?

▲ A basic inscription consisting of initials, with no accompanying ship name or date of quarantine, is almost impossible to research.

▼ A sailor probably took the time to etch this inscription into the sandstone, but without a name to identify the artist, we will never know who it was.

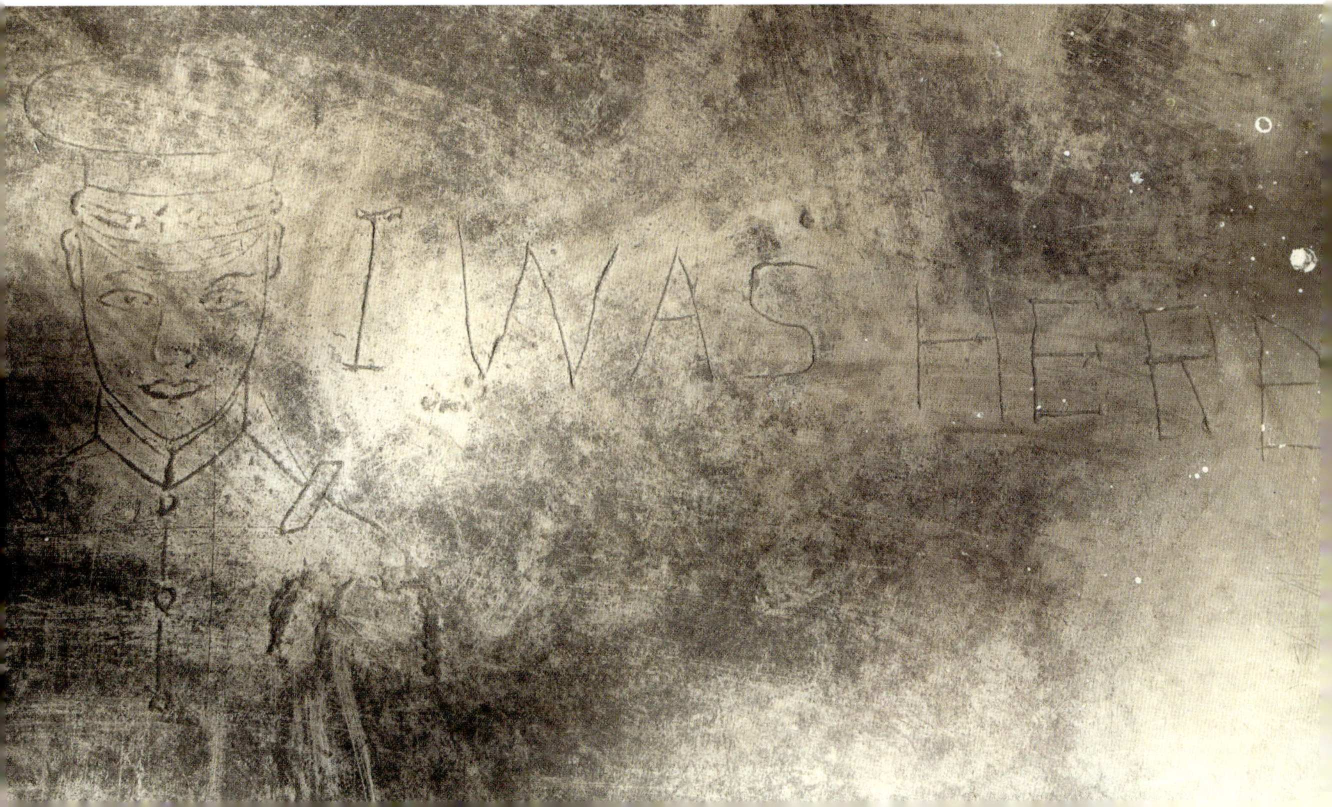

On the ridge line above the Quarantine Station, along a narrow track, a small clearing contains the lonely grave of a six-year-old boy. His headstone is practically all that remains to mark the 102 burials in the Station's Second Cemetery, as most of the grave markers were removed nearly a century ago. Arriving aboard the immigrant ship *Smyrna* on 19 August 1878, Isaac Lowes had travelled from England with his father – a blacksmith – plus his mother, brother and twin sisters. Although sailing to Australia was not especially unhealthy, the main victims of disease en route were children. Indeed, all 13 from the *Smyrna* who died of measles, scarlet fever or typhoid fever were seven years of age or younger. Isaac was buried alongside Thomas Convoy, aged four, whose headstone was later removed but survives in Q Station's Visitor Centre. Another parent who lost a child was Welsh monumental mason Benjaman [sic] Leyson, who probably carved the elaborate panel commemorating the *Smyrna*'s arrival. Once part of the cliff face, the large slab featuring the panel likely fell out due to the actions of tree roots and water; it now forms the boulder that is such a prominent part of Q Station's landscape (see page 83).

An old photograph of the *Smyrna* inscription in situ (far left) reveals one of the reasons for its fall from the cliff face – pernicious tree roots snaked around it and nearby inscriptions.

Although sailing to Australia was not especially unhealthy, the main victims of disease en route were children

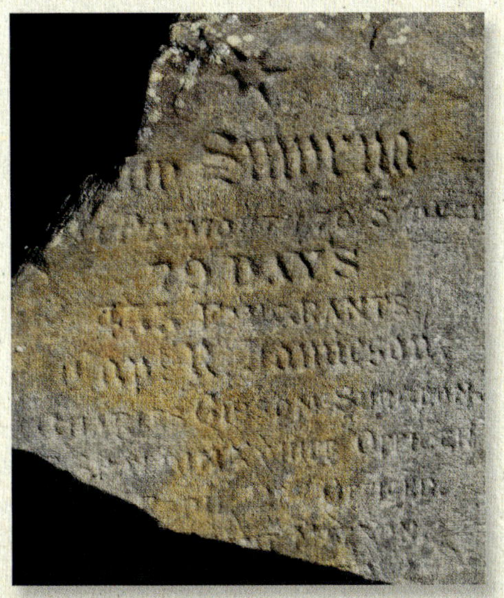

Isaac Lowes's gravestone is the only one that is still visible at the Station's Second Cemetery today. Sadly, Isaac succumbed to scarlet fever on 25 August 1878.

A close look at the *Smyrna* boulder reveals that the inscription was badly damaged even before it fell from the cliff face. Large sections have broken away from the top and bottom.

More than 100 of the inscriptions are in languages other than English – especially Chinese, but also Japanese, Indonesian, Arabic, Russian, Greek, French, Finnish, Fijian, Tongan, German and Italian. And this is not to ignore the special visual language that accompanies many inscriptions, including symbols from seafaring, Freemasonry, military units, various shipping lines and decorative motifs ranging from olive branches to rampant lions and fire-breathing dragons.

More than 100 of the inscriptions are in languages other than English – especially Chinese, but also Japanese, Indonesian, Arabic, Russian, Greek, French, Finnish, Fijian, Tongan, German and Italian

As well as posing mysteries, many of these elements also offer clues. The regional origin of a carved Greek name helped identify the island home of its creator – and what happened to him once he arrived in Australia. Once translated, a Chinese message suggested not only when it was painted onto a cliff face, but the level of literacy and political leanings of its originator. A shipping company's pennant – its unique house flag – helped to identify a vessel, while the 'Speedbird' logo of the British Overseas Airways Corporation (BOAC) marked one of the few aircraft sent into quarantine. Even a partial date next to a name, such as '20 Aug', assisted historians to crosscheck people against shipping lists, newspaper articles, quarantine registers and official correspondence.

◀▶ Inscriptions may show shipping companies' flags, and the design can often be traced back to particular vessels – even if there is no text. These flags suggest the British line P&O (top) and the Dutch company KPM (bottom).

  From Quarantine to Q STATION

ᐱ This Greek inscription at Old Man's Hat features deeply etched letters partly encircled by a traditional laurel wreath design that has almost disappeared.

➤ An engraved dragon forms an important part of the China Navigation Company insignia. The dragon is a symbol of strength and power in Chinese mythology.

ᐱᐱ Finding themselves in a strange land with a language they barely understood, the Quarantine Station's Chinese inhabitants made their own mark on the landscape.

As with the various inscriptions linked to the quarantine of the SS *Chingtu* in 1901, calibrating historical research with archaeological recordings identified not just individuals, but entire episodes carved into the landscape. The arrival of the RMS *Ormuz* in 1901 was one such case; the collection of European immigrants aboard RMS *Orsova* in 1914 was another. Likewise, the quarantine of the RMS *Niagara* heralded a major event: it was the first of over 100 vessels detained at North Head during the influenza pandemic of 1918–19. The controversial quarantines of the *Smyrna* in 1878 and its sister ship the *Samuel Plimsoll* in 1879 were extraordinarily well documented. Yet despite extensive research, the reason why 'J. GENTLEMAN / SCOUNDREL' was elaborately carved into the sandstone remains obscure, even though we know that John Gentleman arrived aboard the *Samuel Plimsoll* in 1879. The search continues. Other individual names recur across the site, including 'LJ Coghlan' – a Sydney resident who was a respected postmaster – as well as those of many members of the MacMahon family, who lived and worked at the Quarantine Station for over a decade.

A Louis Joseph Coghlan (1859–1932) was the Quarantine Station's telegraph officer during Sydney's 1881–2 smallpox epidemic, and his unadorned name can be found in a handful of inscriptions spread across the headland.

➤ The MacMahon family and their friends share a picnic at Spring Cove, *c.* 1951. From 1945 to 1957, family patriarch Frank worked as a labourer at the Quarantine Station.

Finding Meaning

The history of quarantine has always been about much more than simply preventing the spread of disease. It relates to the way that governments have interacted with people – whether their own citizens, new arrivals, tourists or unwanted 'aliens'. Through the building of facilities such as the Quarantine Station at North Head, the process of quarantine also represented a physical embodiment of medical ideas – and the often-disturbing medical realities of illness.

Changes in the Quarantine Station's buildings and landscape, and the ways in which it was reused for isolation, detention and emergency accommodation, are also often mirrored in the inscriptions left at the site. Because it was a place where otherwise unrelated people shared strange circumstances and experiences – whether for a few days, several weeks or endless months – studying these enforced communities tells us much about how people related to each other in the distant – or not so distant – past.

Carving a memory of their presence into the landscape was just one way in which people living through quarantine began a 'conversation' with future visitors to North Head. The 'Stories from the Sandstone' project served to give them voice and meaning.

⋀ One of the most intriguing inscriptions found at the Quarantine Station is an engraving that calls 'J. Gentleman' a scoundrel. Why he was given this villainous label remains a mystery.

⋀⋀ Elsewhere, the name 'J. Gentleman' has been carved by a different hand, perhaps the man himself. John Gentleman, a wheelwright who sailed on the *Samuel Plimsoll* in 1879, bought the blacksmith business of John Bastard in 1885.

⋏ The hospital building (H1), reconstructed after a devastating fire in 2002, overlooks the renovated Wharf Precinct. These once-busy areas of the Quarantine Station are now peaceful reminders of the past.

❯ As part of the conservation process, dilapidated buildings across the Quarantine Station site had cracks and holes in the wood filled before the structures were repainted in carefully selected heritage colours.

Chapter 5

Conservation and Adaptation

The Quarantine Station was transferred to the State Government on 16 March 1984, and came under the management of the National Parks and Wildlife Service. The then Prime Minister, Bob Hawke, and New South Wales Premier, Neville Wran, pledged that sufficient funds would be made available for its conservation as an important part of Australia's heritage. However, the funding never materialised, and the site became the subject of a hotly contested dispute over its future. It soon became apparent that the only option was to find a new function for the site that would generate enough revenue to fund long-term conservation efforts.

What is Adaptive Reuse?

Adaptive reuse plays a major role in heritage conservation in Australia. It involves finding a new use for a heritage site through the addition of a contemporary layer that has a minimal impact on its existing historical elements and ongoing cultural significance. One of the main benefits is that the heritage values of the building or site are protected for subsequent generations – its future is secured because of this new function. Also, access to the original historical building or site may have been restricted, so its transformation into a commercial building or tourism/entertainment venue means that it can be enjoyed and utilised by the general public. Adaptive reuse fosters greater interest in historical sites than if those sites were left untouched, attracting a wider range of visitors than might otherwise have been expected.

The specialised process of adaptation presents many challenges and opportunities for architects and designers to find creative and innovative ways of retaining heritage values while also ensuring that a building will function properly in its new capacity. Requiring the new work to be recognisable (rather than an imitation of the original historical style) and seeking a use that is compatible with the original site are just some of the ways that adaptive reuse can help to safeguard a building's heritage values.

The Boilerhouse Harbourside Restaurant is situated within the Powerhouse (building A6), which once powered the various cleansing processes at the Quarantine Station.

ADAPTIVE REUSE AT THE QUARANTINE STATION

In the late 1990s, The Mawland Group became the preferred tenderer for the Quarantine Station site based on the success of their previous adaptive reuse projects (including Lilianfels Resort & Spa in the Blue Mountains) and their proposal for the Quarantine Station. They intended to adapt the site for the operation of a retreat and conference centre, waterfront restaurant, theatre, interactive tours and education programs. Conserving the site's heritage values was central to these plans, as was adhering to numerous conditions, including the protection of a range of rare or endangered plant and animal species found on the site.

Consistent with the practice of adaptive reuse, much of The Mawland Group's work at the Quarantine Station has not permanently altered the fabric of the buildings and is reversible. For example, to create ensuites for some of the bedrooms, the centre room in a group of three was adapted into two ensuites, each servicing a bedroom on either side through a new wall penetration. The original room size has stayed the same. New ceramic tiles laid in the ensuites add an appealing contemporary layer with minimal intervention – the original floors are preserved beneath the tiled surface.

Exterior works have also required creative solutions to the adaptive reuse of the landscape. One example is the 90-metre elevated staircase built above the original funicular track route between the Wharf Precinct and the Former First Class Precinct. New pathways and courtyards were also integrated into the existing site in ways that both protect and enhance the complex natural landscape while allowing for integrated infrastructure that meets the current needs of the site.

Because of its outstanding national, cultural and historical significance, interpretation and communication of the many stories associated with the site has also been a major goal. The Mawland Group's commendable interpretation program includes the conservation and management of the large movable heritage (artefacts) collection belonging to the Quarantine Station and the installation of a fascinating museum display in the former Luggage Store, which also now boasts a visitor centre and café.

From Quarantine to ℚ STATION

Conserving the Quarantine Station

When the National Parks and Wildlife Service took responsibility for the Quarantine Station, the site was in varying states of disrepair. Many of the buildings had not been used for 40 years or more, and decades of exposure to the elements meant that they had deteriorated significantly. Thanks to The Mawland Group's intervention, this fragile site has been given the respectful conservation that it deserves. The National Parks and Wildlife Service and The Mawland Group remain strongly committed to the long-term preservation and use of the Quarantine Station.

The heritage architectural firm Godden Mackay Logan (GML) guided the project through concept planning up to the granting of planning approval. The GML team helped devise strategies for conserving the cultural heritage of the site, while ensuring that the many challenges and issues inherent in doing so were resolved. Paul Davies of Paul Davies Architects and Heritage Consultants, an expert heritage architect, was then engaged by the National Parks and Wildlife Service to develop the Detailed Architectural Conservation Management Plans (DACMPs). He ascertained the critical area of the site for intervention and conservation, and determined that the most significant building on the site was the Former Third Class Dining Room (now the Governor Bourke Ballroom [P27]), which was to be conserved but not adapted. He was then engaged by Mawland to ensure that the conservation work and adaptation was in line with the DACMPs, and he has continued to advise Mawland on the heritage aspects of the site. Thompson Berill Landscape Design was engaged by Mawland as the heritage landscape architect, and they developed the vegetation and landscape plans, including those for the two car parks and the funicular staircase.

▲ Throughout the project, The Mawland Group has recognised that true heritage conservation is best achieved through securing contemporary use, as seen in this renovated bedroom.

➤ Once used by quarantined passengers as a shower and toilet block, building P8a
is more visually appealing after a coat of paint and a realignment of the stairs.

Thanks to The Mawland Group's intervention, this fragile site has been given the respectful conservation that it deserves

➤ Building A25, used as a post office during the Quarantine Station's heyday,
looked very shabby before meticulous conservation and painting took place.

Conservation of the site has involved many years of slow and painstaking work. In order to proceed with adaptation in any part of the site, it is necessary to have first completed the conservation work. Each unit of work is assessed by the New South Wales Office of Environment & Heritage and the National Parks and Wildlife Service to ensure it complies with a raft of strict conservation requirements. The work is diverse and ongoing, ranging from repairing failed carpentry and joinery in virtually every one of the 65 buildings to painting every building and fitting fire-protection systems throughout the wooden structures. It also involves repairing over 1000 metal, wood, paper and fabric artefacts, including boilers and autoclaves, and repainting faded inscriptions.

Dating from the 1880s, this silver food cover was restored by a moveable heritage conservator. The broad arrow symbol above the 'Q.S' meant that the object was the property of the New South Wales State Government.

Rotting or broken floorboards found on the verandahs were methodically pulled up and replaced with new boards, using the same tongue-and-groove system as the original flooring.

Each unit of work is assessed by the New South Wales Office of Environment & Heritage and the National Parks and Wildlife Service

Conservation of the faded inscription marking the quarantine of the SS *Tsinan* in 1905 involved careful repainting of the lettering and intricate design details.

Rain, wind and visitor contact are some of the reasons why the Quarantine Station's inscriptions are wearing away. Conservators repaint them so the details are not lost.

One of the major conservation works was external and internal painting, which produced some of the greatest visible improvements to the Quarantine Station site and also served to protect the timber buildings from the relentless erosion caused by the windswept coastal environment. The painting was kept within the original colour scheme, although a more vibrant and interesting look for the buildings was created by highlighting small features with strong hues. Paint consultants identified many of the original colours of the buildings, and the roofs were repainted in either grey or red to reflect their

From Quarantine to ℚ STATION

The painting was kept within the original colour scheme, although a more vibrant and interesting look for the buildings was created by highlighting small features with strong hues

heritage colours and to protect the roof substrate. The modern paint dramatically reduces the temperature of the roof, which not only improves guest comfort in summer but also cuts down on greenhouse gas emissions as there is no need for air-conditioning units.

Major maintenance work has also been undertaken throughout the grounds, including cleaning out stormwater and sewer drains clogged with 30 years of tree roots and silt, clearing decades of overgrowth from the edges of existing roads, pathways, buildings and infrastructure, and upgrading aged electrical and communication systems. The conservation work alone is valued at more than $7 million. The cost of the commercial adaptation, fit-out and product development work required to create and maintain the business is not included in this total.

The Future

Q Station, as the site is now called, opened on 25 April 2008. The much greater and more meaningful public access to the site has ultimately led to increased appreciation of its historical significance by the community and tourists alike. Its remarkable transformation from rundown quarantine station to world-class retreat and conference facility has also secured Q Station's future as a viable and self-sustaining heritage site.

◄▲ As the Quarantine Wharf had been infested with white ants and needed to be used as a wharf once again, restoration work required the replacement of much of the heavy timber frame. With the original decking then returned, the work became hidden from public view – like much of the conservation activity across the site.

Transformation Timeline

16 March 1984 – The Quarantine Station is transferred to the New South Wales State Government and becomes part of the Sydney Harbour National Park, under the management of the National Parks and Wildlife Service.

June 1985 – The National Parks and Wildlife Service begins 18 months of major conservation works, including the stabilisation of the most threatened built elements on the site. Historical research, measured drawing of all structures, recording of rock engravings and the cataloguing and curation of artefacts are also carried out.

1987 – Buildings in both the Former Second Class Precinct and part of the Former First Class Precinct are refurbished for use as a conference facility. A guided tour service is established, including the famous ghost tours. However, revenue falls short of that required to properly conserve and maintain the site's unique heritage values.

1988 – An unsuccessful attempt is made to find a private-sector company that would be responsible for the leasing, conservation and operation of most of the Quarantine Station buildings as a cultural tourism destination, subject to strict conservation controls and ongoing supervision by the National Parks and Wildlife Service.

Early 1990s – The National Parks and Wildlife Service again initiates a lease-tender process, this time for the whole site. The preferred tenderer is The Mawland Group, who developed Lilianfels Resort & Spa in the Blue Mountains and whose core business is the operation of hotel schools throughout the world.

January 2000 – A Conditional Agreement to lease is signed with The Mawland Group. Local community members, descendants of detainees and heritage professionals concerned about the future use and long-term management of the site form the opposing Friends of the Quarantine Station group.

▲ Max Player, the Managing Director of Mawland Quarantine Station, has been involved with the transformation of the site since the lease-tender process in the early 1990s.

◀ Cleared of silt and rubbish, the original sandstone-lined stormwater channels can now flow freely. This helps greatly with drainage at the site.

July 2001 – The Minister for the Environment takes the unusual step of becoming a co-proponent with The Mawland Group, signalling the government's commitment to the leasing process. The preparation of the Environmental Impact Statement (EIS) follows, and around 1100 submissions are received after the EIS is placed on public exhibition.

13 October 2001 – The remaining accommodation buildings in the Former Third Class Precinct burn down as a result of vandalism.

7 February 2002 – The 1883 hospital building burns down, with the fire blamed on faulty wiring. This fire and the one some four months earlier highlight the vulnerability of the site and the need for more active use and oversight.

2002 – A Commission of Inquiry is held to ensure that all aspects of potential impact on the Quarantine Station site have been sufficiently considered, and opponents are given a public forum for the airing of their concerns. The Commission of Inquiry then releases its report, finding no major reasons why the project should not proceed, subject to approval by the New South Wales Heritage Office and over 200 conditions.

March 2003 – Following approval by the Heritage Office, the Minister for Infrastructure and Planning announces that the project will proceed.

25 October 2006 – The Mawland Group's 45-year lease of the Quarantine Station site begins, and work commences on the conservation and adaptation of the site.

25 April 2008 – Now known as Q Station, the site officially opens to the public.

Despite the valiant efforts of firemen, who pumped water from the harbour in an attempt to douse the fire, there was little left of the historical timber hospital building (H1) after the 2002 inferno (right). As part of The Mawland Group's conservation endeavours, the hospital was reconstructed (above).

The 1883 hospital building burns down, with the fire blamed on faulty wiring

A photographer from the *Manly Daily* newspaper caught the dramatic moment when the original hospital building (H1) went up in flames.

⋀ Arriving at the former Quarantine Station by ferry is an ideal introduction to the site. Visitors can easily imagine what it was like for the many detainees who were brought here by boat.

➤ Taking a history tour is one of the best ways to experience the former Quarantine Station, as knowledgeable tour guides vividly bring to life the tragic and compelling stories of the detainees.

Chapter 6
Keeping History Alive

Thanks to The Mawland Group's impressive restoration of the site, the once-derelict Quarantine Station has been given new life as 'Q Station', a name that recognises the site's contemporary functions while honouring its past. Alongside Q Station's impressive natural setting and appealing range of accommodation and dining options, it is the opportunity to immerse oneself in the history of the site – which evokes the extraordinary personal stories of so many – that continues to attract locals and tourists alike. Bringing this history to life and encouraging visitors of all ages to actively engage with the site is a range of experiential tours and innovative education programs, alongside the lovingly curated museum.

Stunning Location

Whether visitors arrive by car via the old sandstone archway on North Head Scenic Drive or by ferry at the historical wharf next to the sheltered Quarantine Beach, the iconic Q Station is a breathtaking sight to behold. The buildings occupy what is arguably some of the most expensive real estate in Sydney, with verdant natural bush and heart-stirring harbour views that stretch far into the distance.

Q Station evokes the glamour and excitement of an ocean liner, with astonishing panoramas, a cliff-top perspective on the heavy swells that roll in through the Heads and incredible views far out to sea. The verandahs that skirt the accommodation buildings have the feel of a promenade deck, and the grid of walkways that link the buildings suggests that there is something new and intriguing to discover around every corner.

Q Station evokes the glamour and excitement of an ocean liner, with astonishing panoramas

➤ Originally the entrance to the Quarantine Station, North Head's well-known sandstone archway was later moved to its current location. 'Parkhill' refers to the cottage of the Station's chief medical officer.

➤ Each bright and breezy guest room has been designed to retain its historical authenticity while providing gorgeous contemporary furnishings, videos on demand and wireless internet access.

A Relaxing Stay

First-class accommodation at the former Quarantine Station imitated the quality and exclusivity expected by wealthy passengers on luxury liners. Today, the buildings have been painstakingly restored so that the visitor experience is as authentic as possible. Comfortable accommodation is now available in both the Former First Class and Second Class Precincts, which once teemed with boatloads of immigrants who spent their time socialising, strolling the promenades and escaping to the aquamarine waters of Quarantine Beach.

There are over 70 rooms and five cottages that overlook either the water or the natural bushland of Sydney Harbour National Park. Each room is stylish and contemporary, with superior queen-sized beds and French doors that open out onto personal verandahs. In an ironic twist, a place that was once so isolated from the hub of the city now boasts the best digital devices available, including up-to-date communication systems, flat-screen televisions, videos on demand and high-speed internet connection.

➤➤ The verandahs outside some of the heritage guest rooms at Q Station have seating that allows visitors to relax and enjoy the magnificent views of Sydney Harbour.

World-class Event Facilities

The impressive restoration of heritage buildings throughout the site has allowed Q Station to create a private conference destination with all the facilities required for intimate groups and medium-scale events. The close proximity of Q Station to central Sydney means that it doesn't take long to travel from most offices to a sensational meeting room within a heritage-listed building surrounded by serene bushland and located beside beautiful Sydney Harbour. And events can be distinguished by booking a guest speaker to provide an insight into the history of both the Quarantine Station and the particular room in which the event is being held.

Whether clients are hosting a small meeting or a substantial conference, there is a function room at Q Station to suit any requirement. Two of the most popular venues are the Former Men's Smoking Room and the Former Ladies' Sewing Room, both of which date back to the 1890s. Originally separate recreation spaces for male and female first-class passengers, these two rooms exude the relaxed grandeur of bygone times. Each accommodates up to 60 people and boasts a bright and spacious interior, air conditioning, amazing views and a wealth of modern technology.

▼ Building P12 in the Former Second Class Precinct has been repurposed as a modern function room. Known as the Dr Salter Room, it suits small meetings of up to ten people.

◄ Located in the Former Hospital Precinct, the Nurse Egan Room (H1B) is an adaptable function space. It can be set up with theatre-style seating for 120 people, with round tables for 50, or as a boardroom for 30 guests.

While all weddings are memorable, those held at Q Station are quintessentially Australian, both in terms of the naturally beautiful setting and the deep sense of history that permeates the site. Popular spots for ceremonies include the heritage wharf overlooking Quarantine Beach and the picturesque slopes of North Head, where one imagines generations of newly arrived immigrants experiencing the exceptional views for the first time. Adding to the venue's special charm are the wedding photographs taken on-site, which convey an old-world elegance that is undeniably romantic.

⋀ The Quarantine Station has a long history of weddings, as this delightful photograph from 1948 shows. Q Station aspires to uphold this romantic tradition.

⋁ A modern bride and groom embrace lovingly on the wharf beside the rippling waters of Quarantine Beach. This is a favourite place to take wedding photos.

The luxury and refinement of days gone by continue as couples celebrate their wedding reception in one of Q Station's gorgeous function rooms

The largest function space at Q Station, the charming Governor Bourke Ballroom is open and airy thanks to the lofty ceilings and numerous original window fixtures.

The luxury and refinement of days gone by continue as couples celebrate their wedding reception in one of Q Station's gorgeous function rooms. For a small reception of up to 76 guests, The Dining Room is the ideal location. Originally built in the early 1900s as the staff dining room at the Quarantine Station, this space has been recently refurbished to ensure that it reflects modern tastes and requirements. Larger receptions of up to 180 guests can be held in the heritage-listed Governor Bourke Ballroom, the new incarnation of the dining room in the Former Third Class Precinct. It retains the dark timber floors and high ceilings of yesteryear, and guests can enjoy exhilarating sea breezes from the delightful verandah.

From Quarantine to Q STATION

Dining Options

Dating back to the beginning of World War I, the Powerhouse (building A6) now features two distinct dining options: the Engine Room Bar and the Boilerhouse Harbourside Restaurant. The Engine Room Bar is a casual lunch or dinner location on Fridays, Saturdays and Sundays, and there is a pleasant al fresco terrace that overlooks the gently lapping waters of Quarantine Beach. The Boilerhouse Harbourside Restaurant is open for weekend lunches and daily dinners, and it is the epitome of seaside elegance – with a mouth-watering menu to match. The restaurant often holds special historical dinners, such as Rich Man, Poor Man – a six-course dinner that reveals the very different dining experiences of the various classes during the Victorian period at the Quarantine Station.

For those enjoying the exceptional accommodation or function facilities found at Q Station, the aptly named Views Restaurant offers a delicious buffet breakfast or lunch. Located at the harbour end of the Former First Class Precinct, the restaurant provides diners with impressive sweeping views over the deep-blue water.

➤➤ The al fresco terrace situated just outside the Boilerhouse Harbourside Restaurant is the perfect place to spend a lazy Sunday afternoon, especially when the sun is shining.

˅ Diners at the casual outdoor seating area beside the Boilerhouse Harbourside Restaurant enjoy stunning views of Quarantine Beach and Sydney Harbour's aquamarine waters.

Enthralling Activities

Visitors to Q Station can immerse themselves in a range of different experiences that will allow them to truly appreciate the cultural and human significance of the Quarantine Station. The antithesis of traditional tours, these unique interactive experiences let visitors choose how engaged they want to be. Participants discover what it was like to be a quarantined person, use a paranormal investigation kit or delve deeper into the narrative of the Quarantine Station with the help of a history expert. The interpretive tours will leave an indelible mark on anyone who is moved by evocative oral histories, ensuring that we continue to question our present as well as our past.

ᐯ Participants in one of Q Station's thrilling Paranormal Investigation Nights are introduced to the specialised detection equipment they will be using during the four-hour adventure.

Different experiences ... allow [visitors] to truly appreciate the cultural and human significance of the Quarantine Station

GHOST TOURS

Nightfall becomes the doorway into another world as visitors hear the stories and legends of the former Quarantine Station detainees – especially those who were fated never to leave. For families with children over the age of eight, Ghost Trackers is a two-hour tour that's heaps of fun and only a little bit scary. Ghostly Encounters will captivate anyone 15 years and over with chilling tales of paranormal activity, while Extreme Encounters is not for the faint-hearted – participants spend three hours delving into the darker side of quarantine. Adults who are feeling especially brave can combine a ghost tour with a spooky sleepover in one of the Quarantine Station's most haunted areas.

▲ Flickering lanterns add to the very eerie atmosphere during Q Station's many different but equally engrossing night-time ghost tours.

MUSEUM AND HISTORY TOURS

The former Luggage Store has become a fascinating museum devoted to the history of the Quarantine Station from 1828 to its transformation into Q Station, with plenty of artefacts to bring the stories to life. To learn more about the history and people of the Quarantine Station, visitors can take one of the two history tours – the 45-minute Quarantine Wanderer, or the two-hour Quarantine Station Story. Highlights include vivid retellings of the personal stories of quarantined passengers and the dedicated staff who lived and worked on site, the autoclaves that were used to sterilise luggage and personal effects, the inhalation chambers, the hospital and doctors' and nurses' stations, and much, much more.

▲ Q Station's museum includes reconstructions of First Class and Third Class ship cabins from the RMS *Niagara*, which was quarantined in 1918 during the pneumonic influenza pandemic.

Austere and utilitarian, the third-class disinfecting showers have changed little since they were last used by those quarantined due to contagious disease.

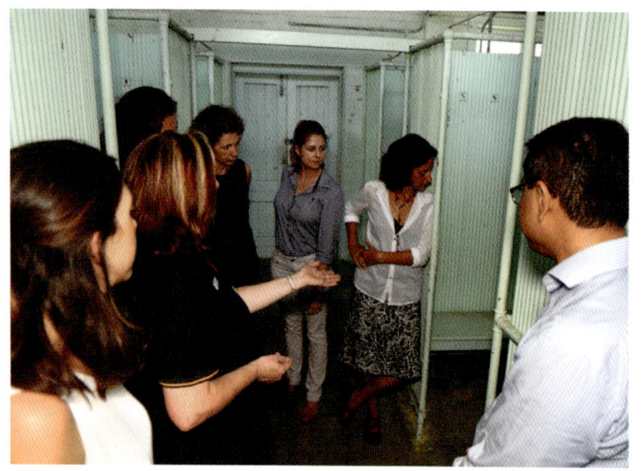

Highlights include vivid retellings of the personal stories of quarantined passengers

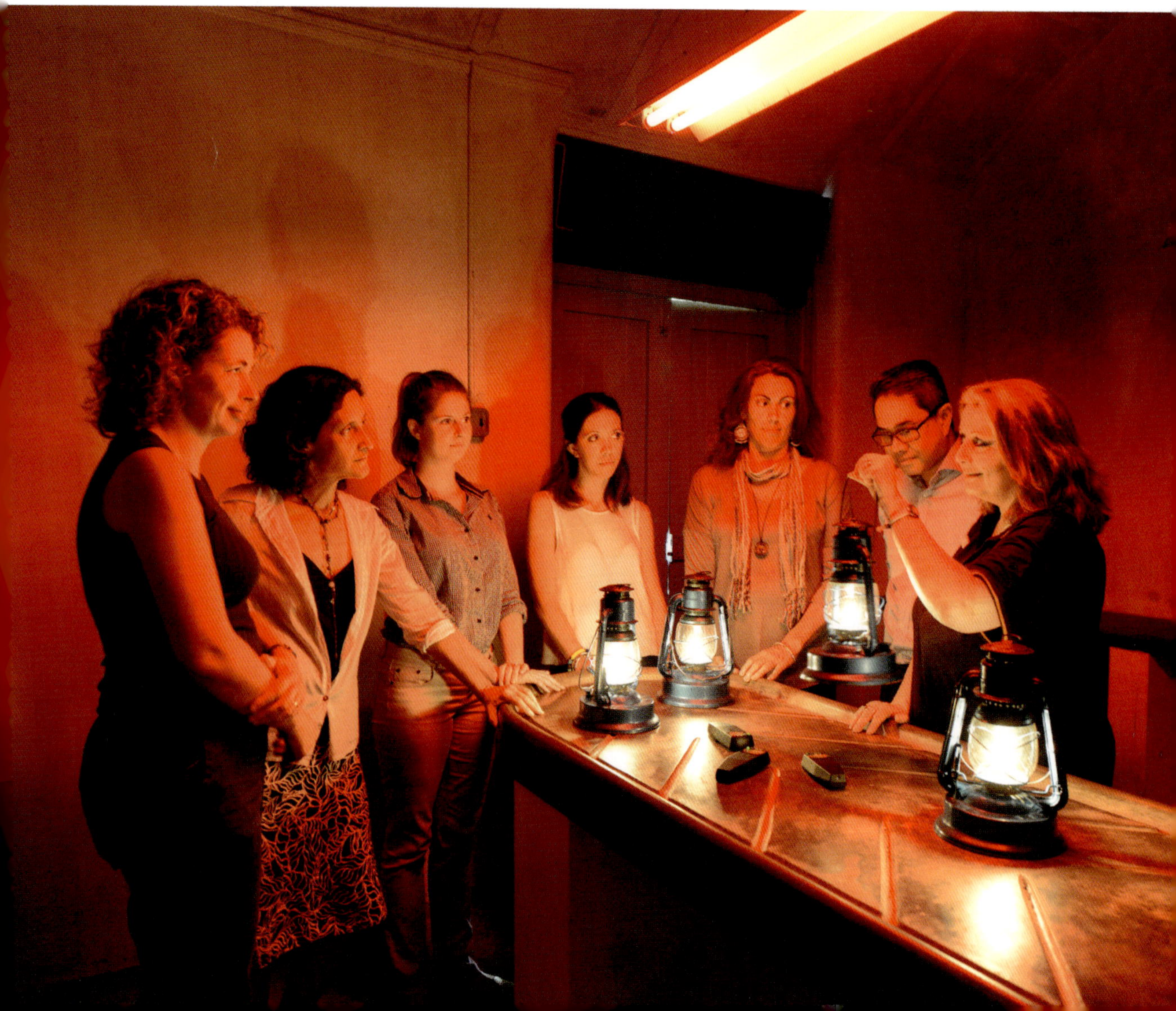

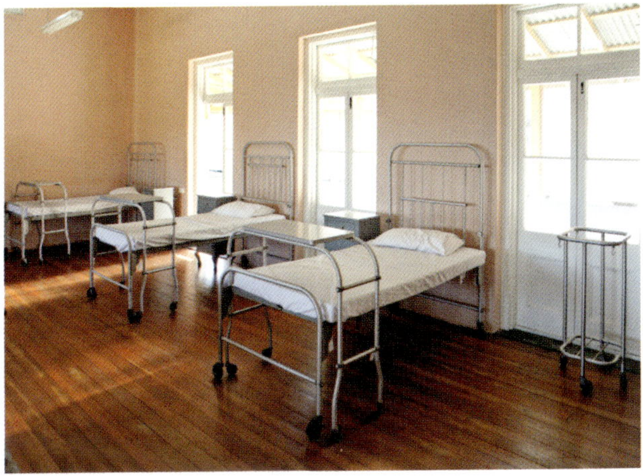

△ History tours often visit the reconstructed hospital wards, where visitors can wander past the old beds and imagine what it would have been like for sick detainees.

◁ One of the most unusual places visited on the ghost tours is the morgue, also known as the mortuary. Some visitors claim they can feel a presence in this building.

△ Oozing old-world style, the guest lounge is the perfect place to read and relax. It offers everything from 1920s maritime novels to a computer for surfing the internet.

▽ Tour guides reveal how the two large autoclaves – now more than 100 years old – were used to sterilise the luggage and personal effects of quarantined individuals.

TEAM-BUILDING EXERCISES

Q Station offers a range of team-building activities to suit each client's requirements. A fabulous way to bond while exploring the history of the Quarantine Station is Outbreak! The company is 'quarantined' due to the outbreak of an unknown disease, and team members must work together to find the required survival equipment, solve puzzles to identify the virus and then come up with a strategy to collect the necessary vaccine.

Other corporate team activities run by third-party companies at Q Station include Human Scrabble and Raft Race, as well as events inspired by the television shows *Survivor* and *The Amazing Race*. For a unique perspective of the Q Station site that is guaranteed to create energy and enthusiasm among team members, single or double kayaks can be hired to explore the stunning Q Station coastline.

Education Programs for Schools

A number of education programs for school-aged students, each accompanied by a teacher's resource kit, explore curricula through the history of the site as viewed from a contemporary perspective. The most popular program to date is Ghost Boy, inspired by the children's book of the same name written by Felicity Pulman. Ghost Boy takes students on two

◀ Children of all ages are fascinated by the Ghost Boy program, as they discover what it was like to live through the smallpox outbreak that occurred in Sydney in 1881–2.

Education programs ... explore curricula through the history of the site as viewed from a contemporary perspective

time-zone journeys that contrast the past with the present, encouraging kids to contemplate the future.

Another interesting program, known as 40 Days – based on the original length of time people were quarantined – is an interactive experience that asks students 'What would happen if you were quarantined tomorrow?' This program allows students to compare medical and communication technologies from 1918 with those of the present, to reflect on changing issues of class and race, and to think about the concept of freedom – all while flexing their drama muscles.

▲ Visiting the diverse buildings throughout the Quarantine Station and hearing the intriguing stories of the detainees breathes life into the history of the site for high-school students.

Acknowledgements

This book draws heavily on the work of Lady Jean Foley, who has been researching the history of the Quarantine Station for many years. Her book, *In Quarantine: A History of Sydney's Quarantine Station 1828–1984*, was published in 1995 and remains the major work in this area. The extract from Charles Moore's diary, edited by Rob Wills, can be found in *Human Hopes: The Diary of Charles Moore*, which was published in 2005 (Moore was an English immigrant to Australia on the *Constitution*). We gratefully acknowledge the review of the Aboriginal Heritage chapter by the Manly, Warringah and Pittwater Historical Society, and the development of the A Natural Place chapter by the Directors of Thompson Berrill Landscape Design.

Picture Credits